HURLING HAKA

By

MIKE NAPIER

ISBN: 978-1-7394550-0-2

First published 2014, updated 2024.

CHAPTER 1

Ben couldn't believe what he was hearing. He looked around the class at the faces of his classmates hoping that he hadn't heard correctly. But no! They were all looking shocked as well. This couldn't be right. It just couldn't be. This was going to be his year. He had been sure of it. He had been all psyched up to have the best year of his life. But this had ruined his day. Maybe even ruined his year? Liam was sitting beside him, and Ben could see tears escaping from his eyes. Paddy just kept saying …no, no, no …like as if it was the only word he knew. Adam was cursing under his breath. Yoda wanted to be sure of what he heard.

"Mr. Fitzpatrick. What did you just say?"

"I said that, unfortunately, the school would not be taking part in the under 12s schools hurling competition this year."

"But why, why, why..." the sad, almost tearful, chorus came up from the class.

"Guys – I told you already. There's nobody to coach. It's as simple as that. I'm sorry but that's the way it is."

Mr. Fitzpatrick handed back control of the class to Mr. Vance and left the classroom. Mr. Fitzpatrick was the Principal of Ballincastle National School, and he had the unenviable task of informing fifth and sixth class that, for the first time in the history of the school, they would not be fielding a team in the 'Sciath na Scol' hurling competition. He had delivered the bad news and left the classroom quickly. Mr. Vance was left to pick up the pieces of the devastation that was visible in every girl and boy player in the class. There was shouting of unfairness. There were tears. There was banging of desks. Hurling was a serious business in Ballincastle National School. Even though it was a really small school, and they were usually pitched against much bigger schools – they wanted to have the opportunity to play. Sciath na Scol hurling was the high point of the year, and it was unthinkable that they would not be entering a team. It had never happened before.

Mr. Vance explained again that Mr. O'Connor, who had trained each team that came along for years, had had a serious accident on his tractor and his leg and hip were going to be in a plaster cast for months. The school had tried to get someone else to stand in for him for this year's competition and take over the coaching of the team. But everyone was too busy and could not spare the time during the day to take on the coaching duties. The number of teachers in the school had been cut by the Department of Education so no-one on the teaching staff was able to take on the task. They had asked Mr. O'Connor if he might know of anyone from his circle of friends or people he knew in the sport – but he had come up blank.

"It's not fair."

"It's not right."

"Why our year?"

"Stupid bloody tractor."

"There must be somebody."

"We probably would have won this year."

"Yeah."

"Let's coach ourselves."

Mr. Vance tried to get some silence and control back into the class but there was such disappointment and uproar that he did the only sensible thing – he let the class go out early to the playground for their first 'small break' of the day. Unlike the usual stampede that accompanied the classroom exit for small break - the boys and girls of fifth and sixth class filed somberly out through the classroom door and towards the playground square. There was a lot of muttered discontent as the different groups got together in the yard. Usually, the girls hung around with the girls and the boys tussled with the boys. Today the recent revelation had completely changed the playground dynamics. It had now changed to hurling playing groups – regardless of gender – and the remainder. Kate, Vicky, Sue and Ceara were in the middle of the boys' group and they were being even louder than the loudest boy.

"This can't be true."

"How can they do this to us?"

"Adults – they can't be relied on to organize anything."

"Mr. Fitzpatrick didn't try very hard before he pulled our team out."

"Have the teachers no pride in Ballincastle?"

"This can't end here."

"Agreed – this is a crock if ever there was one."

As they spoke and shouted over each other it seemed impossible that any one of them could hear the other. But by a biological miracle it seemed that each and every one of them absorbed, filtered and understood every last word. Denial had fed anger and anger was starting to break into determination and resolve. The group that was returning into the classroom was slowly morphing into a pretty gritty bunch. By the time Mr. Vance called them all back into class they had already set themselves up for action. This wasn't called the Rebel County for no reason. This province didn't have a Munster motto of 'Stand Up and Fight' for no reason. This wasn't going to be accepted. This was a challenge. This needed action.

It was Ben who issued the call to arms.

"OK. Let's think about this until 'big break'. Then we come together again. Are we together? Are we agreed?"

Big break was the name given to the lunch time recess. The next two hours of Maths (long division), English (some stupid poem) and Irish (awful grammar) passed by very quickly. There was very little attention paid. Some of the non-players took up the responses in the class as the players mulled over how this thing could be fought. Eimear, Sam, Mark, and Gerry played a blinder – diverting and answering Mr. Vance's questions and letting the others have the time to think things through. For them the two hours dragged as they suffered with remainders, rhyming verses, and future tenses. For the hurlers – the time flew by as if they had just sat down.

"OK class. Lunchtime. I am on playground duty today. So – no messing out there. Be careful and look out for each other."

Oh yes. They would look out for each other all right. Today – of all days – they would be united together. Already the non-players, by answering all the questions in class, had shown they were willing to take one for the team. Without being asked they had done more than anyone could have expected of them. Never before had the whole class been united in pursuit of the same target. Not in the school Christmas play. Not in the school's athletics competition. And certainly not in the school choir. No – this was the important one. This was where every boy and girl was now being tested as to whether there was metal below the surface. Whether this was TTTKA or whether this was a case of INUCOSM. This was a time where hidden talents would develop. Where strengths would be tested. Where leaders would begin to emerge.

The same groups got together again. Two hours of thinking of nothing else besides how Ballincastle National School could field a team in the Sciath na Scol schools' competition without having a coach to train them had yielded a big fat zero. Oh yeah – there were suggestions OK. Suggestions that had as much chance of success as an icicle in Hell. It was nearly time to go back into the classroom – big break was coming to an end. They were getting frustrated with the stupidity of some of the suggestions. They were starting to fight with each other. Insults and accusations were starting to fly. The team resolve was being threatened by the frustration of not coming up with anything reasonable.

"What kind of a suggestion is that?"

"GYHOOYA"

"Are you for real?"

"Who told you that you had a brain?"

Mr. Vance was rounding them back into class.

"Stop. Stop. Stop. This is getting us nowhere,"

It was Ben who tried to pull them together.

"In two minutes time we will be back in class. In another two hours' time we'll have parents, grandparents and child-minders dragging us into cars, separating us and bringing us home. This needs quick action. Who is on WHATSAPP?"

There was a show of hands.

"Right. 7pm this evening. The most important WHATSAPP session of our lives. Be there. Whatever you have to do – be there. Don't be late. And don't screw it up – don't lose your electronic privileges. Behave when you get home. This is too important to screw around with. Best behaviour. We'll have a plan by tomorrow. I promise you. Any problem with this?"

There was a silent shake of the head.

There was a silent line back into class.

Later there was a very silent pick up of fifth and sixth class students by parents, grandparents, and child minders.

There were some exceptionally well-behaved children between the hours of 2.40pm and 7.00pm.

The most important WHATSAPP communication session of their short lives would commence at 7.00pm.

CHAPTER 2

Since Ben had suggested it – it seemed natural that he should take on the role of facilitator. He was the one who started asking the questions, evaluating the replies, and keeping people in line when they started bickering amongst each other. He'd never been in charge of a WHATSAPP conversation before – in fact he didn't think anyone of his class had ever 'been in charge' of a WHATSAPP conversation before. WHATSAPP wasn't that sort of thing. He had really enjoyed WHATSAPP ever since his Dad had brought him back an iPAD mini from New York. His Dad travelled a lot. His Dad hated his job and mostly because of the travel and missing his family. He used to like his job but the only way he could hang on to his job was to do all this travel. Ben didn't like the fact that his Dad was away either – but hey – the iPad Mini was a compensation. Every time his Dad travelled, he came back with other stuff – baseball bat, baseball glove, American football, books, sweets (apparently Americans call them candy?), cool clothes. Well – it was a decent compensation!

But this WHATSAPP conversation – this was unreal. Before this the conversations had been reasonably calm. This was getting out of control. As the texts started to fly uncontrollably back and forward - he thought of what his Dad had said to him about his Dad's rules of 'WHATSAPP-ing'..........

1. Do not use bad language.
2. Beware sending photographs.
3. Be aware that you leave a permanent record – you can't use your usual excuse that you didn't do it – the record is there for everyone to see.
4. Do not bad mouth anyone – this is cyber-bullying.
5. Don't ever join in cyber-bullying.
6. The brave boy is the one who says – let's stop the 'bad mouthing' and talk of something else.
7. I want my son to be the brave one.

OMG. Godammit. This was the time that his Dad had talked about. This was the time he had to be brave.

He WHATSAPP-ed.

"STOP."

"STOP."

"STOP."

"Are we a team r wot?"

"CMIW – but we need 2 stand 2gether. Need to support each uder 2 get thru dis. Need 2 b a team. Who do u think u are? A skool of teachers? We need solutions not problems."

The last one was something he heard his Dad say. He wasn't sure if it was right in this situation, but it didn't sound too far off the mark.

There was a very long WHATSAPP silence. Very long.

Then Vicky WHATSAPP-ed.

"OK. YYSSW."

Not much of a support. But Vicky had always been a supporter of his and tensions were running high. Probably the best he could hope for in relation to calming things down.

There was another long WHATSAPP silence. Ben wasn't sure if the whole thing was falling apart. Time was marching on. He was conscious that his Mam and Dad had very strict bedtimes of 9.00 pm. What a bloody nuisance. Sooner the better he was older and could go to bed anytime he liked. Now he was battling against his own bedtime clock and every other WHATSAPP participant's bedtime clock. Absolute bummer being a twelve-year-old having to go to bed when you are told.

The WHATSAPP conversation went back and forward. In fairness – it was a lot more restrained and positive since Ben had made his intervention. But they knew they were all up against the bedtime final whistle and suggestions were beginning to get a bit frantic. One player (who will remain nameless because they would not want their stupidity to be recorded forever) actually suggested bringing in the Global Commissioner for Human

Rights. Another player (who will remain nameless for the same reason) suggested that a case could be brought to the Supreme Court. Yet another player (yeah! – nameless as well) was of the opinion that the Irish Constitution might protect the rights of Ballincastle hurling players (either going to be a future lawyer or a raving idiot).

It was getting close to 9.00 pm. Ben was having trouble keeping it all together. OMG. There were rubbish suggestions coming from all over the shop. He hated having to put in those awful letters – GTG-BI-ALL. But it was getting very close. His Mam was hovering and had given him a three-minute warning. His Dad was backing her up. This was not going well. He was going to have to sign off soon or be kicked off (no pun intended).

Then came the breakthrough. Noel came good with the immortal WHATSAPP...

"The Parents Association should help us."

Of course! That was it. Mr. O'Connor was out of the equation. The teachers couldn't do it. But this was exactly the type of thing that the Parents Association could take on.

There was only time for one last WHATSAPP before Ben's parents manhandled him down to the bathroom to wash his teeth.

"Noel – you beauty – perfect – lets bash our parents to get PA to get us back in."

CHAPTER 3

It worked!

But in a way that none could have imagined if they all lived to two hundred and fifty. The Parents Association had their regular meeting and they agreed that it would be a shame if the school wasn't represented in the Sciath na Scol schools hurling competition. They trawled for a replacement coach. They had problems filling the gap for the same reason as Mr. O'Connor and the schoolteachers. But ... eventually they succeeded. They canvassed all the parents and their friends and all the friends of their friends. And they got a volunteer. As it happened it was a father of one of the Junior Infants class.

Now – Junior Infants is the starter class in school. The girls and boys (well – babies really) are around four years old. So – none of this class are going to be challenging twelve and thirteen olds for a place on the Sciath na Scol hurling team. So – why did this Bruce person volunteer? Well – allegedly – he is a sporting person – a new member of the PA – and somebody who couldn't bear to see a sporting team not represented. Well done Bruce. Oh yeah – Bruce has recently moved to Ireland from New Zealand. And yeah – Bruce is a (as you might expect) – rugby person. And also – Bruce doesn't know a hurling stick from an umbrella. And as for a sliotar – to him it is a foreign language – but it is also as far from his experience as a snowball at the equator.

So here they were…all togged out…on the practice field…the Ballincastle National School Hurling Team…boys and girls…just thankful to be in the groove…with hurleys and helmets…ready to go…waiting for Bruce to put the team through their paces…waiting for…

"Hi Guys and Gals."

Muted Hi.

"My name is Bruce."

Slight delay.

"Hi Bruce."

"I'm looking forward to getting to know each and every one of you."

Nothing.

"I don't know squat about hurling. But - hey - it's a ball game – all ball games are pretty much the same – aren't they?

Definitely nothing.

"I'm a rugby man. OK. I'm a New Zealander – which means the same thing – rugby man. Ball game – same thing. Yeah?"

Silence. How can you get less than 'definitely nothing'? Tadhg had his mouth open so wide that no fly was safe.

"So – let's start with some basics – yeah?"

Eyebrows were raised. What the hell planet is he from?

"Pride in the jersey – yeah? Understand one thing – you are only minding this jersey for the one that comes after you. It's not yours. You have the privilege of owning it now. But this is only temporary. There is someone else coming up and he or she will wear it prouder that you ever can. It's life. It goes on. But this is now. And now you have to mind this jersey like your life depends upon it. You have to keep it for as long as you possibly can. You have to defend it. Defend it against the next person who wants it. Have you pride in the jersey? Have you pride in yourself? Are you with me?"

Ben looked at Vicky. Paddy looked at Liam. There was a soft kind of response. It obviously didn't satisfy Bruce. Because the next activity was definitely one that was never – ever – seen on a Ballincastle hurling field before.

"Ka Mate Ka Mate

Ka Ora Ka Ora

Ka Mate Ka Mate

Ka Ora Ka Ora

Tenei te tangata pu'ru huru

Na'a nei tiki mai whaka whiti te ra

Upane ka upane

Upane ka upane

Whiti te ra

Hi!"

Heads looked around. Looking at each other. Looking into space. Some looking at Bruce. Some not knowing where to look. OK – this was different. This was way out there. And - let me tell you about some words that definitely do not go together. Soft and HAKA. Relaxed and HAKA. Laid back and HAKA. Peaceful and HAKA. Calm and HAKA. By the time Bruce was finished with the team on their first training session with him – the players knew nothing additional about hurling

– but they had the smell of blood in their nostrils.

Bruce said that just to make this different, to make it something unique and special, to make this clear that this was their statement - that they would call it the HURLING HAKA. Wow. This could be a complete and unmitigated disaster, or it could be the start of something completely new.

"WHATSAPP @ 7pm guys – let's get your opinions on what the hell is going on here!"

CHAPTER 4

The post training analysis on WHATSAPP was interesting. There were a lot of different perspectives. Ben tried to keep it all together or at least with as few conversation threads as possible. But try coordinating this lot:

Paddy: I liked Bruce doin de HURLING HAKA – I'm lookin 4ward to leadin it.

Vicky: Bruce has cute body.

Liam: I don't know how we ur goin 2 improve ur hurlin skills.

Kate: I luv his accent.

Robbie: I'm goin 2b the one leadin de HURLING HAKA.

Vicky: Who wud u rather kiss –
Bruce r Matt Damon?

Fionn: Any1 know what we got 4
homework?

Adam: I'm proud to be an All
Black.

Sue: At least Bruce is far better
lookin than Mr. Fitzpatrick or Mr.
Vance or Mr. O'Connor.

Ben gave up.

Ben: GTG CYA 2moro.

At school the following day the
talk before school, in the playground at
small break and at big break, was all
about Bruce and Sciath na Scol
training. A few of the lads had googled

the HAKA the previous night and every so often you could hear someone break into a random 'Ka Mate, Ka Mate'. It was a bit of a laugh really. A subgroup of girls – Ceara, Sue, Vicky and Kate – had formed to mark Bruce out of ten and see where he ranked in the league table of Paul Mescal or the One Direction lads. The boys tried to stay as far away as possible from that rubbish. They were wondering what was going to happen in the next training session and it seemed as if it was going to be a long week until next Wednesday's session.

But it wasn't. The week seemed to fly and here they were again – all togged out on the training field waiting for Bruce to arrive. He arrived togged out in his All Blacks kit.

"Right guys and gals. How is everyone this afternoon? Everyone firing on all cylinders? Ready to explode out of the blocks?"

There was a kind of muted 'yeah' like as if people were muttering something under their breath. You know – where your Mam or Dad tells you to go to bed and you mutter something not quite nice at a volume that they are not one hundred percent sure what you said and what they heard – that kind of volume.

"Oh no, players. This won't do at all. How can we prepare when you've left most of your heart back in the changing room? No. No. This won't do at all. Follow my lead guys. Do as much as you can. You'll soon have it off by heart.............. Ka Mate, Ka Mate."

Some of the guys weren't actually that bad at doing it. Probably the same guys who had been doing the Googling during the week. Others resembled Sumo wrestlers with haemorrhoids. The girls definitely had not got a clue. Kate, Ceara, Sue and Vicky had gathered in a girls-only bunch and there was more tribal war dance ferocity in Swan Lake than their pitiful rendition. Still – Bruce seemed encouraged that everyone shook an elbow, or a knee and he had a big broad grin across his face.

"Guys and Gals – that was super stuff for a first time. I've known New Zealand school teams who wouldn't have done such a great job on their first time around. I've a really good feeling about this squad. Yes mates. I can feel it in my waters that you guys are going to do the business. Other teams are going to quake with fear when you guys take the field. It's a banker."

The players all looked at each other. Any similarity between what had just been done and the HAKA seemed entirely accidental. Still – Bruce was the New Zealander around here – so he must know what he was talking about.

"Now we are going to do an exercise that really challenges your teamwork and your ability to work for each other. This is called rucking, mauling and passing."

With that Bruce pulled out a rugby ball. He took one half of the group and called them rugby forwards. Then he took the other half of the group, nominated one of them as scrum half and told the rest of them that they were rugby backs. The essence of the exercise was for the forwards to link together, gather around the ball, walk over it and then the scum-half to pass the ball and then person-to-person along each of the backline while running up the field. Last person puts it down on the ground and the forwards are all supposed to be there and repeat the exercise in the other direction.

There was a lot of muttering under breaths...

"If I wanted to play rugby, I would have joined the Rugby Club..."

"If my Da caught me playing rugby he'd kill me."

"This is bloody crazy – we're supposed to be practicing our hurling skills."

"If Mr. O'Connor could see this...

"This is mad..."

Of course, the first few times were a complete shambles. The backs dropped the ball, the players were in front of the ball, the forwards stood still and didn't know what to do, and people bumped into others or fell over each other. For at least the first ten attempts, even picking up dropped balls and continuing, the ball didn't make it to the end of the line. The pace was so slow that the looping forwards were colliding with the backs making them drop the ball or fall over. But Bruce persevered. After about twenty minutes the first flawless passing movement resulted in Paddy placing the ball down on the wing for the forwards to bind together and drive over.

"Super – I knew you guys could do it."

There was a lot of back slapping and high fives.

"Now let's see that rugger ball really travel out the line and all the forwards ready to drive over once it hits the ground. Kate – you go in scrum half. Ben – you go in outhalf - and get that back line organized. I'm told that you are the usual goalkeeper. Well - you'll be used to shouting at your backs and getting them organized. This is no different – make sure that they are lined up behind you in a sloping line ready to run onto the ball. And be ready to move to the far side of the pitch behind your backline once you've done your pass. And really shout at them. Everybody needs to be clear where you want them."

By the end of the session the group could go from one end of the pitch to the other – going right, going left and then going right again. People were even beginning to showboat and dive over for tries. As the light began to fade Bruce called them all into the center of the field in a circle around him.

"Now that was really something guys. You are really beginning to work for each other. Really beginning to click as a team. Next week we are going to do something special."

He paused. No-one said anything. Clearly, he was waiting for the obvious question. But they were already learning the HURLING HAKA. They were already training like a rugby team. What could be the something special? Eventually Ceara spoke up and asked what they were going to do.

"Next week – guys – (pause, pause, pause) – we are – (pause, pause, pause) – going to play – hurling!"

There was a couple of seconds of quietness and then the cheers broke out.

"Brill."

"Bout time"

"Way to go."

"Totes amaze balls"

They filed off the pitch in small groups.

"WHATSAPP tonight lads. 7pm.
Get yourself in the groove. Talk later."

CHAPTER 5

The WHATSAPP sessions were getting larger and harder to control. Those who previously didn't have access to WHATSAPP were somehow finding powers of persuasion in their homes to be allowed to access. It had turned into a fairly massive on-line conversation with no rules and little structure. Ben had given up trying to put any shape on it. It was impossible. It was just going to go where it was going to go. Sub-conversations within sub-conversations were taking place – a thread had become a web. Sport, fashion, 'fitness' tables, truth or dare sessions, schoolwork – it was all there and more. Usually by 9.00 pm the participation began to dwindle as people were hunted towards teeth washing and beds. Ben really resented the fact that he was driven off WHATSAPP at 9.00 pm. Why did he have to go wash his teeth and prepare for bed at 9.00 pm when others in his class got to WHATSAPP around until after nine? It wasn't fair. What he really didn't like was not being the last one to sign off WHATSAPP. It made him feel more childish that others could keep online and be bouncing stuff off each other while he was sucking Colgate. Misery. Every night a misery.

Schoolyard talk was still dominated by Bruce's training techniques. And it wasn't just the schoolyard. Robbie had overheard Mr. Vance and Mr. Fitzpatrick talking about the fact that some of the parents had complained that they didn't agree with rugby balls being used for hurling training sessions. There were still some parents who regarded rugby as an English sport and that didn't go down well in certain households. Apparently, it was all to do with history and politics. Whatever that meant. Noel's mum was on the Parents Association Committee, and he said that Bruce's training techniques had been discussed at the PAC meeting and also at a Board of Management meeting. Sue had another bit to add. She said that Mr. Fitzpatrick had been asked to get Bruce to drop the rugby stuff – the HURLING HAKA, the rugby ball, the All Blacks speeches. Word was that Bruce had politely told him that they had asked –

no begged – him to coach the team, and if they didn't like his methods then he would happily stand aside and let someone else coach. When there was someone else nominated, he would pass over the coaching baton - but up until then he would continue and he would continue the only way he knew how. Cool. Bruce was taking a stand, but his wagon train was slowly becoming surrounded by injuns. And some of the other natives were getting restless.

Every training session was now eagerly awaited by the team. So, the following Wednesday they all took the field wondering what was going to happen next. Bruce arrived on time as usual and got them all collected in the center circle.

"Ok – this session let's have one of the girls to lead the HURLING HAKA. Kate – can you take the honour? Ka Mate, Ka Mate..."

Kate did a fine job as a lead. She had obviously been doing a bit of you tubing. All of the others were getting better as well as each session gave another opportunity to practice and show off.

"Now – this week we promised some hurling. So, let's have a practice match. We'll divide into two teams - listen up while I call your names..."

"Team one – Ben in goals, backs Iggy and Tadhg, half backs Ceara and

Paddy, center Shane Mac and Kate, half forwards, Vicky and Liam, forwards Eoin and Fionn.

Team two – Robbie in goals, backs Noel K and Sue, half backs Damian and Shane C, center Adam, half forwards Ted and Malcolm, forwards Jack and Noel O'B."

Everybody looked at each other in amazement as they strapped on their helmets and took their positions. Bruce had called out all their names. First bit of amazement – he had done it without having to read them from a list. Second bit of amazement – and much more important – he had broadly positioned them where they were best used to playing. Wow. He had done his homework. Bruce blew the whistle, retreated to the sideline to watch and just left them at it. He was not going to even try and referee the match. After the first couple of minutes they started making their own decisions as to fouls and wides and sideline cuts.

Astonishingly the match was relatively well conducted and didn't degenerate into complete bedlam. OK at one stage Malcolm had to be dug out of Ted but they were actually on the same side. Apart from that it was all pretty tame. Bruce came on to blow the final whistle and Team One had run out comfortable winners by 4-12 to 1-8 but a lot of that was down to Ben playing a blinder in goal for Team One and the fact that Team One had an extra player. Apart from that it was a more even contest than the score line suggested.

It was at the after match warm down that Bruce dropped a bomb shell that none of them had been expecting.

"Guys – I have some news for you…"

A low murmur ran around the group. So, this was it. The parents had had their way. They were all expecting him to say that someone else was taking over the training from next week. The looked around quickly one to another. There were long faces all around. This had been fun. This had been different. Even today – that they had been allowed to conduct things themselves – even that was different.

Oh well – back to the old ways for next week. Probably doing boring laps of the pitch. Each of them wondered who it was that had been forced into coaching to replace Bruce. Probably somebody boring who would just shout at them and think they were coaching.

"...Next week..."

Go on. Say it. Get it over with. Mr. So and So will be taking you for training...

"...There's been a change..."

Yeah. Guessed it.

"...To the schedule..."

Get on with it.

"We play our first-round match. It has been brought forward because of fixture clashes and availability of grounds."

What! No one knew what to say. Bruce was still their coach. That was good. That was fun. But next week? They weren't ready. They were far from ready.

"Sorry guys. I can't pronounce the competition. What is it called again?"

"Sciath na Scol."

"Yeah – Ski Na Skull. That's it. We are playing Duncoiste. And I promise you and I promise them. They won't know what hit them when we are finished playing them. Now together guys – Ka Mate, Ka Mate."

CHAPTER 6.

The WHATSAPP session that night was mad. Everybody was connected and everybody wanted to text at the same time. Some of the WHATSAPP-ers were filled with doom at the prospect of playing Duncoiste next week. Duncoiste were a pretty good side. Rumour had it that they had some really big players who weren't slow to throw themselves about and didn't take any prisoners – male or female. One of the guys who had a cousin at school in Duncoiste and who was playing with them also said that they had been training every week for the past eight weeks. There were a lot of pessimistic guys on the call who reckoned they hadn't had enough training under their belts and that they would be whopped.

Others, including Ben, were more optimistic. Most of them played with clubs outside of school and had been playing now for a good number of years. They had strengths. They had a decent panel. They needed to play to those strengths, but they could take Duncoiste. Their hurling skill level had advanced hugely over the last couple of years. Their catching was better, they could solo, and they could pick a man out rather than hit and hope. They could work off each other and for each other. At the last practice game Liam had scored a point directly from a sideline cut. They were much better at foiling the opposition by a well-placed hook. And they could play their way out of defence and through the midfield to make sure they retained possession. They all had their different capabilities and strengths and of course there was always room for improvements, but they weren't carrying anyone.

It was a stated aim of the school that everybody on the squad was to get a run out in the competitive matches. So, for every game there would be a panel of at least sixteen picked – eleven starting and seven substitutes. Sciath na Scol team numbers of eleven were different from routine hurling team numbers of fifteen – presumably to help smaller schools field a team. The bench had to be emptied for every match – the five subs would each get a run out in the game even if it was only for a few minutes. And by the time the competition was finished every squad player would need to have seen some action. This generated huge differences in opinion within the team. Some of the squad believed that the school should always put out its best available eleven and then only ever substitute tactically. Some of the parents (the ones who thought that the 'taking part' principle was only for losers) also supported the best eleven approach. But the vast majority of parents supported the 'playing time for all' attitude and they were very vocal about it. Nobody was quite sure where the Principal Mr. Fitzpatrick's heart lay in the debate, but it didn't matter, because he had his arm severely twisted by the equality band of parents.

Paddy: "Not fair. We shud put out de best XI."

Sue: "Don't agree. We all train. We all do ur best. We all shud get chance."

Noel: "That's just cause u wouldn't get a game otherwise."

Ben: "Easy der. Easy der."

Tadhg: "Agree wit Paddy. Because we small school we av 2 mix frm 6th class, frm 5th class and even frm 4th class. The other bigger schools don't need 2 do dat. They all 6th."

Eoin: "Yeah – so we at disadvantage immediately. They'll generally all b bigger than we are."

Ben: "Not big that matters. Hurling about skill. Remember. That's why we play it."

Adam: "Yeah. Yeah. But big and skillful eats smaller and skillful 4 breakfast vry day."

Sue: "Not necessarily."

Adam: "Ah yeah. Sometimes. Sometimes not. But u know wot I mean. If they are all bigger it has 2 help."

Ben: "We're still going 2 take dem. Even if we have 2 run under their legs. We're going 2 take dem guys. Agreed?"

The number in the call started to diminish slowly as 'Colgate Time' drew them away. Ben tried as many delaying tactics and shouts of unfairness as he could muster but eventually he had to give in .....

Ben: "GTG CYA 2mrow."

A number of the remainder stuck out for longer until eventually they were down to Paddy and Noel.

Paddy: "We are going 2 win aren't we?"

Noel: "Ka Mate........

Schoolyard talk resisted every other topic for the next week. Even the non-playing class members got sucked into the frenzy that became the lead up to the first Sciath na Scol match of the season. Mr. Fitzpatrick said that the Parents Association would pay for a bus to take anyone from third, fourth, fifth or sixth who was interested in supporting the school team at the match. The squad themselves were going to have their own twenty-four-seater bus just for them. There was a fever beginning to grip the school. Anyone with a relative or friend attending Duncoiste school was conscripted as a spy to find out anything they could about the Duncoiste Sciath na Scol team – what kind of backs, forwards, midfield did they have? Did they normally play it out of defence or bang it up the middle? Who were their danger players? How many girls did they usually play? Was it best eleven or empty the bench? Were they tall? How good was their free taker? Would they go for points or goals? Who had they beaten recently? Who had beaten them? How had they beaten them?

There was initially what seemed like good information that came back from the spies but there was also some weird stuff beginning to creep in. Within a couple of days there were stories of epic proportions that just couldn't have any basis in reality. It was hard to believe that a team of twelve-year olds could all be over two meters in height, each weigh one hundred kilograms and every one of them capable of doing the hundred meters in under ten seconds. And that was just the feedback on the Duncoiste girls! After a while it became hard to separate the good stuff from the weird stuff so the guys just stopping asking.

The days were counting down. It was time to stop thinking of Duncoiste and time to start thinking about Ballincastle. Nothing was going to change the fact that they had to get off to a winning start and they had to play whatever monsters appeared against them in the Duncoiste School strip. Roll on the game. Once the sliotar was thrown in and the whistle blown they would know very soon where they stood.

CHAPTER 7.

The day of reckoning had come.
First match in Sciath na Scol. First of
three matches and then whoever
topped the group would go into a
semi-final. Four good games and then
they could be striding out in Pairc Ui
Rinn in Cork City for the final of Sciath
na Scol. Or lose today and probably be
out of the competition. In principle you
could still lose one game and advance
to the knockout stage but it meant the
other teams would have to take points
off each other. Better to keep your fate
in your own hands and just keep the
wins ticking over.

The boys and girls who got on the
white minibus outside Ballincastle
National School all had butterflies in

their stomachs. There were very few breakfasts eaten that morning. Very little attention had been paid to carbohydrate loading because there were a lot of team players who just had no appetite for food. Or who were afraid that it wouldn't stay down. The first match was always the worst. Once you got one match under your belt it would steady the nerves. But now there was a nervous edge to the banter on the bus. It was like as it everyone's voice was a little higher pitched than normal, the laughs were longer and out of proportion with the joke, the fidgeting was viral.

Bruce had brought a big bag with him onto the bus and plonked it beside him on the front seat. Nobody had paid much attention to it but halfway to the ground he stood up in the aisle of the bus (despite the driver trying to get him to sit down) and started asking for hush while at the same time opening the bag.

"Guys and gals let me interrupt you all for a couple of minutes. I know that for as long as anyone can remember Ballincastle have played in a blue strip. Nobody was able to tell me where the blue color originated from or whether it has any significance. So today…"

Bruce started taking a set of gear from the bag.

"…today – Ballincastle Ski na Skull strip changes to all black."

Bruce held up a set of gear – black jersey, black shorts and black socks.

"There is one for every member of the squad and I know you'll wear this strip with pride. More than that – I know that by wearing this strip you will be able to draw on another ten percent that you didn't even know you had. An extra ten percent that will mean the difference between winning and losing. And when you have put this strip on, and you look at your fellow players in the dressing room you will be prepared to do anything to help them. No player will get isolated – he or she will always have a support on their shoulder. No player will lack someone to pass to – they will need to make choices as to who to pass to. No player will defend or attack alone – there will always be layers of back up. You guys are the best. Play like the best. I won't say anything further when we get to the pitch. This is it. It's up to you guys. Same players who were on Team A at training start the match. Tadhg leads the HURLING HAKA today."

There was a strange silence where noises got magnified. The revolutions of the bus engine now sounded so loud and enveloping. Players looked at each other. Was he serious? Were they really going to perform the HURLING HAKA before a hurling game? Wasn't this just a training ground ritual? Tadhg was looking at everybody – searching for some sort of reaction. A nod to say, 'go ahead my son'. A twist of the head to say, 'not on your nelly'. There was nothing coming back. Nobody knew how to take this.

They were still totally confused as they got the new all black gear on in the dressing rooms. It did feel really good though. It had those slinky panels in the jerseys that felt like nothing they had ever touched before. And the shorts felt like silk. And the socks when pulled up to the knee and folded over had them all looking like a class act. Sue made some silly comment about black being so slimming but the look of thunder that was directed her way soon stopped that kind of conversation.

Meanwhile Bruce just leaned back against the dressing room door with one knee bent back under him against the wall like he was cool as a cucumber. The time had come. It was time to take the pitch. Tadhg was still looking around him for someone to mark his card. If he twisted his neck with any greater frequency his head was likely to come clean off. They got up to go. Tadhg couldn't take any more. He looked over at Bruce.

"HURLING HAKA now?"

His voice had a quiver in it like when you know you are about to do something, you are not entirely sure if it is right, and you have this sneaky suspicion that you could bring an unmerciful bucket of crap down on yourself.

Bruce looked him straight in the eye without moving a muscle.

"Tadhg – take them to the center of the pitch. Own the center of the pitch. You are today's leader. Think of nothing else other than providing that lead. You are in the zone. There is nothing outside of the zone. Everything after that will flow."

Tadhg hadn't a clue what he was talking about. But they were to do the HURLING HAKA. That was all he wanted to know. He led them out to the halfway line. Everybody knew at this stage what they were supposed to do. They moved arm's length away from one another in two roughly equal lines. The Duncoiste team was all gathered around one goal pucking the sliotar around. Tadhg took up a position facing them and started to vibrate his hands...

"Ka Mate. Ka Mate..."

The Duncoiste players started to smile at first but as they saw the intense looks of the Ballincastle players the corners of their mouths started to slowly creep down. After a couple of verses of the HURLING HAKA there was an eerie silence all around the pitch but once they had finished and leaped into the air there was a massive roar from the Ballincastle supporters – pupils and parents together.

Tadhg looked around at his fellow players. There was no uncertainty now. It was game on.

CHAPTER 8

The bus on the way back to school was a riot of sound. Everyone was sharing their favorite memory of the game. And the HURLING HAKA came way up there in the league table of memories. It is true that after the match some of the Duncoiste School Team people were talking about complaining to the County Board but at that stage nobody was paying much attention. Duncoiste had been good. They had been very good. OK so they weren't all two metre, one hundred kilo speed machines – but they were all skilled athletes, and on another day, they might have hammered Ballincastle. But today everybody played out of their skin. Subs and all.

Duncoiste scored a point, then Ballincastle would get one back. Duncoiste would grab a goal, then Ballincastle would stick one in the net. It was also true that Ballincastle had to work harder each time to get their scores, but they were willing to keep the pressure on, whatever it took to do that. Midway through the second half there were the beginnings of a crack within the Duncoiste Team. They were getting frustrated that they couldn't shake Ballincastle off. No matter what they did Ballincastle kept coming back at them. The strain on Duncoiste was starting to show. A wide shot that they would have nailed in the first half, a missed hook, a halfhearted effort to compete – the signs were evolving of a Duncoiste team that were finding the going that little bit outside their comfort zone and their experience.

It was five minutes before the end before Ballincastle led the game for the first time. But once they got a nose in front, they knew they were not going to leave it behind. It was still incredibly close and there was only one puck of a sliotar in it at the end – 2-14 to 2-13. But what a game! What a victory! Every point was replayed on the bus back to the school. Each of the goals became more heroic with every telling. Saves that were made, hooks that were put in, catches and intercepts, shoulders and tussles, ground hurling, soloing – there were never more heroic episodes than that last sixty minutes of interplay. Players were openly praising each other for the individual part that each had played. Paddy and Liam had been the ones who had hit the net and others were queuing up to recreate each interplay with them and relive that second where the sliotar rippled the net. Equally well - at the other end-the saves that Ben had made became more dramatic and more gravity-defying with every cycle of recollection.

Some of the parents who had attended the match had attempted to take their children back home in the family cars. Every player stood firm and whinged at hurricane level nine until they were allowed to get the team bus back to the school. This was too good a day not to be in the thick of the celebration. In between the stories from the battlefield there were short interruptions of songs and chants. But no-one could keep up the interest in singing for very long and it would inevitably revert back to the tales of epic bravery with which each one of the Ballincastle warriors had been involved. The journey back to the school was too short. It seemed like they had just left the pitch and now the bus was pulling off the main roundabout, taking the corner at the church and pulling to a halt outside that stone building which had first taught students over one hundred years ago.

As the driver turned off the engine, Bruce stood at the door and pulled himself up to his full height to round off the day with his own post-match analysis. He started his words with an historical approach.

"You will be remembered for what you have achieved today in an All Blacks jersey. Future students will tell the story. Parents will tell the story. Teachers – here today and in the future – will tell the story. The day the Ballincastle hurling team took to the field in All Blacks jerseys, performed the HURLING HAKA and pulled off a stunning victory. Make no mistake. We are making history. You were exceptional today. But it doesn't end here. No. Not by a long shot. It only ends when we get our paws on that Ski na Skull trophy. That is when we make real history. And that will be for the rest of your lives. People will stop you in the street in fifty years from now and ask were you part of THAT team. The classes in front of you guys and behind you guys will ask themselves why they were born when they were and missed out on the chance of a lifetime. We've started a journey here and we're not going to slow down or stop until we reach the destination and get our prize. And that destination is Ring Park. And that prize is the Ski na Skull trophy. You are amazing. Now...look out that window. You have got children and teachers and parents who are so proud of you. Look at their faces. I want that look on their faces etched into your brains. Because this is the beauty of giving it your all. It's not always winning. Sometimes the bounce of a ball or a 50-50 decision can be the difference between winning and losing. But this is the look of pride. And pride is the real winner. So...we are going to open the bus door and you are going to give them all the loudest scream of your life. Because we mean business."

Bruce was just about to get the bus driver to open the door and everyone had their mouth half open to scream when Bruce turned around again.

"Oh. And don't forget training next week."

Each team member was like a fully inflated balloon ready to scream and by the time the door opened there was an ear-splitting roar that came out of the bus. What surprised them all was the massive cheer than returned from the kids and parents. This train had well and truly left the station.

Getting off the bus they all went their separate ways to the cars and school buses that were lined up to take everyone home. As they spanned out Ben let out a yell from the car window.

"WHATSAPP tonight 7.30pm for anyone who can make it. This we absolutely need to talk about."

All the way home in the car Ben felt he was floating on air. On the journey he couldn't stop talking about the match, the goals scored, the goals saved, every play in the game. It was easily the best they had ever played.

He kept talking seamlessly as they got out of the car, in through the front door and inside the kitchen. As his Mum walked the dog around the garden (pees and poos), he followed her around reliving every wonderful moment of the afternoon. He was still remembering bits and pieces when he suddenly saw the clock on the mantelpiece and realized that it was already WHATSAPP time. By the time he had opened the programme the conversation was in full flow.

Paddy: " Yo Ben. Good of u to join us. Wassup?"

Noel: "Yeah. Wot were u doin Ben? Why the delay joinin us. Were you lookin for a pro contract or wot?"

Ben: "LOL. When ur good ur good. Wassup wit u lot?"

Vicky: "Just njoyin the buzz."

Sue: "And wot a buzz. OMG. Were we totesamazeballs or wot."

Kate: "Bruce went 2 another planet."

Tadhg: "We played like we wur out of dis world."

Ceara: "Yeah u guys in Mars, we gals in Venus."

Adam: "WTH. Anyone know wot she's on bout?"

Kate: "Oh we know. We know. Cant help it if u boys r so slow n don't understand."

Ben: " Y. And uve told us so often. Now can we get back 2 match?"

Malcolm: "I am so lookin 4ward to next round."

Fionn: " Any1 know who playin?"

Ted: "I heard dat we will b in paper 2morrow."

Daire: "Wot paper?"

Jack: "Guy from Echo der."

Robbie: "Aah. Better if Examiner."

Iggy: "Who cares. Picture in paper gud."

Damian: "Who said picture?"

Eoin: "Doh! Cameraman!"

Adam:" I didn't see ny cameraman."

Ben: "Gud man. Proves u wer focused."

Eoin: "U sayin i wasn't focused?"

Shane: "Down boy. Back in ur box now."

Ben: "Getting whacked wit a toothbrush. BCNU. TTYL."

CHAPTER 9.

School the next day was nearly as good as the match. All the junior kids wanted a piece of the players in the playground before class started. When the students assembled in the classroom the teachers led a round of applause and Mr. Fitzpatrick gave a speech saying how proud the school was of the huge effort that everyone had put into the game. All of the players were standing a little taller by the end of the day. During small break and big break there was only one topic of conversation whether you were a player or not. It had been confirmed that the two next games would be against Baileleara and Rathairne. The radars were out, and the antennae were up to find out as much as possible about the next opponents.

By afternoon an illicit text had been received that confirmed that their picture and a small write up was in the Evening Echo. The phone with the text on it was passed discretely under each desk from one to another. Not surprisingly there was a mention of the 'war dance' that was done before the game. If the Echo had it then all the local weekly papers would have it for their weekend edition as well. Tadhg reckoned that as HURLING HAKA leader the papers would probably be queuing up to interview him. He wondered if it was too soon to get an agent. Kate was sitting beside him and when Mr. Vance turned his back, she gave him such a massive big pinch on the arm that he had to suck in hard to stop himself howling with pain.

"What's up with you Tadhg?"

"Nothing Mr. Vance. Nothing at all."

"Well sit up straight and pay attention."

Kate smirked. Tadhg whispered that she was one dead child. Class went on and soon revenge was forgotten as everybody funneled down towards 2.40pm and towards the freedom bell. The usual madness accompanied the exodus from the class. Now there was an extra incentive to get out and get a parent to buy the Evening Echo and see the photo and read what was printed. Ben ran out towards the classroom door not caring who he knocked over in the process. His brother Leo spread himself in a big X in the doorway to put a stop to his sprint. A brief tussle ensued before Ben broke himself free and across the yard. He spotted his Mother with a newspaper under her arm. Good on her. He ran over and yanked it from her arm.

His Mother looked at him - "Well good afternoon Mam. And how are you Mam? Did you have a good day Mam? And thanks for getting the newspaper for me Mam. You are such a thoughtful Mother. I don't deserve you. I really don't."

"Yeah, yeah, yeah. Thanks Mam. What page is it on?"

Ben was frantically leafing through the paper, sometimes turning multiple pages at one time, and having to reverse his way through the paper and then onwards again. He must have gone through each page twice before he found what he was looking for. It was a bit disappointing really. It was a tiny photograph, so small you couldn't really distinguish anyone clearly. There was even a photo of the Duncoiste team. What did they want a photo of the losers for? And the write up was pretty sparse. Some sentence to say that the crowd was treated to a war dance before the game and then a couple of additional sentences...tight game...very little between sides in the end. Well that report certainly burst their rising balloon for sure. Ben was expecting a full page. Even half a page. Not a couple of weeny pictures and a miserable few sentences. Pity Tadhg had already been collected by his Ma. He could have rubbed it in hard about the interviews with the HURLING HAKA leader.

Oh well – onward and upward. As soon as Ben got home, he got out his training rebounder from the shed and set it up. He had got this for Christmas – it was like a taut vertical trampoline that you pucked the sliotar against – the trick was to control it again as it bounced – sometimes in an unexpected way – back towards to you. Truth was he had hardly played with it since his Dad assembled it on Christmas Day – but now he felt he should be out doing some hurling practice whenever there was daylight. He wanted to improve his reflexes, and this was a perfect way to do it. He'd also get his brother to fire shots in at him, but this was up close and personal and required much greater speed of reflexes.

He beat shot after shot after shot into the rebounder before his Mother called him in to eat. It was only then that he realized that his Father was home and that it was almost dark. He felt so tired that he reckoned he'd give his nightly conversation on WHATSAPP

a skip and take an early night – and
that was saying a lot.

CHAPTER 10.

The next couple of weeks just seemed to go by in a haze of activity – training, more training, practice games and then the second Sciath na Scol game. They played Rathairne and, while it wasn't an easy victory, they closed out the game very well. Unlike the previous game, they took a lead in the first quarter of the game, and they were always four or five points to the good throughout the game. A final score of 3-12 to 0-13 flattered Rathairne. The backline and Ben in the goal were on fire and there was never going to be a sliotar in the Ballincastle net on this particular occasion. Rathairne were reduced to picking off points from frees and from out the field. Liam, Eoin and Malcolm shared the goals.

Kate had led the HURLING HAKA and she led it with as much passion and conviction as any of the boys had done previously. The Rathairne team had been a bit bemused but the Ballincastle crowd roared it on and the local papers carried a photo of Kate doing the final leap of the HURLING HAKA.

Now here they were on the pitch in Baileleara. Baileleara was always renowned for having a tall and physically robust team. Must be something in the water of this town. Bruce had rotated the HURLING HAKA lead to Paddy for this match and for some reason it didn't seem as explosive this time around. The Baileleara team had obviously read about, or got wind of, the Ballincastle HURLING HAKA exploits and they arranged themselves on the halfway line almost breathing down on Paddy's neck. If they weren't so physically big then maybe it would not have made much difference. But some of the Baileleara guys were huge. I mean some of them looked like they had beards and moustaches. And that was just the girls!

So maybe the Ballincastle team wasn't as fired up as normal from the impact of the HURLING HAKA – but whatever the reason – Ben had a pain in his back in the first fifteen minutes picking the ball out of the net three times. There was nothing he could do to stop them. Baileleara were ploughing through his defence as if they weren't even there. When half time came the team were just happy to get in off the pitch and regroup. They had never had so bad a start. They were down 3-5 to 0-6 and Baileleara looked good for every goal and point that they had scored. To make matters worse Baileleara had also beaten Duncoiste and Rathairne so this was a winner takes all game. Even a draw would not be enough for Ballincastle because Baileleara had a much better score difference from their two games. This was looking like the end of a dream and the long faces; the bent heads and the dragging legs of each team member told its own story.

Bruce let them settle down a bit and get some water on board before he tried to raise their spirits.

"OK guys – these boys and girls are big, guess there must be hormones in the Baileleara beef. And yes, they've built up a lead. But what do you think they are saying to themselves now? Any ideas?"

No-one had the energy or the inclination to say anything – even if they had an opinion.

"I'll tell you what they are thinking, and I'll tell you what their coach is saying. They are thinking they have this won and their coach is telling them to keep doing what they are doing – more of the same. And do you know what – when they step out for the second half – they are going to be complacent, a little bit cocky, maybe a little lazy, definitely not fully focused. You on the other hand are going to blitz them away in the first five minutes. Go at them so hard they won't realize what or who hit them. You are not going to hold anything back – nothing. Don't worry about energy to last the full half – I'll look after you with substitutions – empty the entire bench at the one time if necessary – change the whole team if I have to. Empty your tanks completely – because you will have no need of that energy if we lose this game. This is it guys. This is your final. It is not going to end here. You will go out there and play like guys and gals possessed. You have the skill level of champions. You have the energy levels of winners. And you have the belief of heroes. Do it."

Before the referee blew his whistle the Ballincastle boys and girls were balancing on the balls of their feet just waiting for the off. Once they got the signal they tore into the game. They hunted like a pack of lions, they sprinted like greyhounds, and they were as tenacious as terriers. They supported each other in waves when in possession and they swarmed around each Baileleara player when dispossessed. Bruce called it spot on. Within five minutes Ballincastle had clawed two goals back as well as a scatter of points. Inevitably they had given away a number of frees with this high-octane game and Baileleara had gratefully kept their end of the scoreboard ticking over. Twenty minutes into the second half the pressure of being run manically around the field began to tell on the Baileleara players. They were surrounded on each occasion on all sides by Ballincastle players – backs and forwards alike. When they did break free, an almost physically impossible stretch would hook the sliotar from their attempted shots or clearances. Any ground hurling was dominated by the Ballincastle never-say-die attitude. Some of the Baileleara heads were looking distinctly sweaty and combined with bright red faces and puffing cheeks, they were looking markedly more uncomfortable as each minute progressed.

Bruce kept his word and started putting on subs in groups of twos and threes. There was no letup in the tempo. Guys and gals ran themselves into the ground until they were physically not able to cover another blade of grass and Bruce watched them all like a hawk and called them ashore before they spent themselves completely. Ballincastle hit a purple patch on the twenty-five-minute mark when Bruce had refreshed the line up with three subs together and accompanied by a few positional changes on the pitch as well. Within the space of four minutes Ballincastle had played the sliotar up the park twice and rifled shots into the Baileleara net.

Ten minutes to go and the sides were all square at 4-10 to 3-13. Baileleara were still picking off points from frees and this was keeping them in the game. Both sides were feeling the effect of the speed of the game and even though Bruce had rotated every single sub into the game there were still some very tired legs out there. Both sets of supporters were giving it welly – cheering, roaring and screaming every facet of the play of their side. Neither team deserved to lose this game but Ballincastle couldn't have it end as a draw. To go out of the competition that way would just be too much to bear.

Each side traded a couple of points in the last few minutes. 4-12 to

3-15. Attacks were breaking down on each side due to pure tiredness. Mistakes that usually would never be made were happening repeatedly. The two teams had worn each out physically and mentally. But Ballincastle were running out of time. With the time almost up Ballincastle had a sideline cut well into the Baileleara end of the pitch. Jack was getting ready to take it but then beckoned Liam over.

"Liam – what's the chance of you pointing it directly from here?"

"Don't know. Edge of my range."

"Look – go for it. The ref has looked at his watch three times. Just keep it on target. At least if you're short we might have the chance of a flick on."

Liam took his time selecting the best tuft of grass and placed the sliotar three different times until he was absolutely happy that it was sitting as proud on the grass tuft as it could. He bent down on his hurley and sliced into the ball for all he was worth. As he lifted his head up he was happy that he got the direction right. Everybody – players and supporters alike – watched the flight of the sliotar as if time was standing still. It didn't look as if had the legs. Then if looked as if it just might have the legs. It was close. Maybe too close. Even if it did make it the distance, the goalie might still be able to stop it going over the bar. Liam lost sight of the last part of the flight as hurleys were stretched up in the air from attackers and defenders alike. A flag went up and there was a massive roar from the Ballincastle supporters. Liam wasn't sure whether he had cut a point directly or not, but he didn't care. They needed to pack the defence now for whatever was left. They just had to defend that point.

Baileleara threw everything bar the kitchen sink at them for the last two minutes. Where did the ref get two additional minutes from? Ballincastle matched them with the ferocity they had shown in the opening section for the second half. Tackles went in without concern for life or limb. Players suddenly found reserves of fuel even if they had been running on fumes for the last while. Baileleara were trying to play in close to the Ballincastle goal because no Baileleara player was going to take responsibility for a 'hit and hope' knowing that the ref would probably blow up when the sliotar next went out. Ballincastle were feverishly trying to hunt them out of their half of the pitch.

Eventually the ref blew.

Baileleara players just lay down on the ground totally dejected. Some Ballincastle players did the same totally drained. The subbed Ballincastle players ran on and dragged everyone to their feet. There was a massive huddle in the middle of the field with everyone jumping up, jumping on each other, jumping like they had all just got a new lease of life. Someone tried to get Liam shoulder high, but it was quickly abandoned due to lack of energy and strength. Liam took this as confirmation that he had pointed it.

"Was it my point?"

"You better believe it you little beauty."

They were in the semi-final. One step away from Pairc Ui Rinn. Life didn't get much better than this. But it could. It really could get better. Roll on the semi-final.

CHAPTER 11

This time the local newspapers were overflowing with coverage of the match.

"Ballincastle qualify for Sciath na Scol play offs."

"Ballincastle edge out Baileleara in tense decider."

"HURLING HAKA inspires Ballincastle."

There were photos of the team, photos of Paddy leading the HURLING HAKA, and one of the papers had got hold of a photo of Liam in mid swing when he cut the point. Tadhg was getting a lot of good-natured slagging about his previous statements of being interviewed for the papers. Now it was

Paddy who was getting all the attention, although no one was exactly looking for media interviews. There was a great buzz around the school, and they were all waiting patiently to see what the draw was going to be for the semi-final and who they would have to face.

They didn't have to wait long. News galloped on the grapevine that they were to face Carrigleann and that the match was to be played in Watergrasshill. There were whispers and rumours and crossing of hearts. There were denials and questions and rejections. But eventually Noel produced an official looking piece of paper with G.A.A at the head of it and it confirmed their opponents and the venue. They knew that the further they got in the competition that there would be no easy games. Still they had had some fairly stern tests along the way, and they had got this far. They had to feel they were in with a shout.

Noel: "Don't matter who dey are. We'll beat nyway."

Ben: "Spoken like a true All Black."

Ceara: "I heard dat Carrigleann won all der games well."

Vicky: "Well!?! They crushed de schools dey wur playin gainst."

Iggy: "Dey made mincemeat of dem."

Sue: "I herd it was embarrassing. 1 skool didn't score gainst dem at all."

Adam: "Wot? U mean not even 1 single point?"

Sue: "Not a sausage."

Daire: "Whoops."

Eoin: "Oh oh."

Ben: "Hey guys. Stop talkin em up. Dey r probably havin de same conversations bout us."

Practice was still a mixture of hurling practice games and rugby training moves. The players were getting as good at spin passing, rucking and mauling as they were at soloing, ground hurling and hooking. There were still elements of disquiet from some of the parents, some of the Parents Association, and some of the

School Management Board with Bruce's methods. There were factions who were openly critical that rugby balls, rugby moves, and that rugby HAKA had absolutely no place anywhere near a hurling pitch. There were others who brought up old history and asked was this what the founding fathers of the State had given their lives for? They shouted to anyone who would listen to them that this was absolutely not what the Gaelic Athletic Association was created for. Fact was, though, that most of the parents weren't listening. Bruce was getting results and filling the kids with self-belief. That was good enough for most parents.

Whatever the sides that were taken – every adult around Ballincastle was united in one belief – they wanted a day out for themselves and their children in a Sciath na Scol hurling final in Pairc Ui Rinn in Cork City. Everyone dreamed of sitting in the stand and cheering on the Ballincastle School team. Interest levels were certainly beginning to peak, and Bruce's training sessions were actually beginning to attract a crowd. This wasn't all good. Parents who before had not expressed any opinion one way or another on the practice of the HURLING HAKA were now being drawn into a debate.

Nothing changed before the game at Watergrasshill and Bruce still gave his pre-match encouragement on the bus on the way to the game. They all knew the prize that was ahead of them were they to win today's game. Some of the team privately would have been happy just to be in a final even if they didn't win it. They also knew that you wouldn't dream of saying such a thing to Bruce. Others were desperate, now that they got this far, to go all the way.

Bruce finished off his pre-match speech:

"...and remember this. People remember winners. They may recall runners-up. But nobody ever remembers semi-finalists. Ceara – let's

go to the girls to lead today's HURLING HAKA. Let's do this thing."

They were all more quiet than normal in the dressing room. Everybody seemed to be thinking their own private thoughts. However, when Ceara took to the middle of the pitch and started the now familiar quivering of the fingers...

"Ka Mate, Ka Mate..."

...it became a different story. Eleven players became bonded in a mission that had one single purpose. They took their positions up and down the pitch and there was a knowing look exchanged between them all. It said - I'm ready. It said - I'm with you. It said - you can rely on me.

The whistle blew and the ref threw the sliotar between the midfielders. Right from the start Shane was on to it and Ballincastle were making the running, stroking the sliotar between them with confidence. They played across, forward, back with patience until Damian put Liam into space and he struck a glorious point over the bar. The game was on and Ballincastle had laid down a marker. From the puck out Vicky made a glorious catch picking the ball out of the air with all the ease of a county player. She tipped it on to Liam and he put his second point on the board in as many minutes. It was a brilliant start and the Ballincastle crowd roared them on.

Unfortunately, that was to be end of a very short purple patch. Carrigleann settled down and started to show that you don't win all your games in the qualifiers without being a quality team. They put a number of flowing moves together and started to dominate all the breaking balls, forcing themselves physically into the game. Before long they had snatched the two points back, added another three points and then in a particularly sickening end to one of their attacks the sliotar came back off the crossbar and a 'Carrig' hurley was on hand to force it over the line. Twenty minutes gone and Ballincastle were down 1-5 to 0-2. Twenty minutes down and Ballincastle hadn't pointed in eighteen of those minutes. They were beginning to look ragged and impatient and out of control. Mistakes were being made. Passes were missed. Puck outs were being hurried. Lifts of the sliotar that normally would have been taken with ease and confidence were now being fumbled and dropped.

Bruce was on the sideline with his two hands out - palms down - appealing for his charges to calm things down and take their time. In his usual fashion he was calmness itself with no shouting or roaring. The same could not be said for the Ballincastle crowd who felt that the more they shouted, the louder they roared that it would somehow change the fortunes of their sons and daughters. It didn't. 'Carrig' kept moving the sliotar with ease from backs to half-backs, through to half forwards and full forwards and picked off another three points. In goal Ben was roaring at his defence at the top of his voice that they were leaving their opposition to roam free and not marking closely enough. If they didn't do something soon this match was going to be out of sight with no way back.

Ben took a sliotar, exchanged his goalkeeper hurley for his puck out hurley and went to the edge of the square to look for his target player. Usually he splayed it out to one side or the other. He felt he had to try something different. Nothing was working. He put his hurley straight up in the air and hoped that the team got the message that he was going straight up the middle. He let rip with all his strength. He connected perfectly and the sliotar sailed through midfield and as far as the half forwards. Eoin managed to win a brief ground hurling fight and touched it on to Malcolm who just pulled on it and it flew into the top corner of the net before the 'Carrig' keeper even knew what was happening. It was a lifeline at a time when Ballincastle were drowning in 'Carrig' pressure. Heads automatically came up. It kept the scores better behaved. They fought harder, ran faster and covered more ground than before. It was just the pick-up they needed. They managed to keep 'Carrig' scoreless for the rest of the half. A half time score of 1-8 to 1-2 flattered

Ballincastle. It could have been so much worse.

Despite the goal that kept them in touch it was a tired team that walked towards Bruce. The heads were still down when they huddled together for his half-time talk. Bruce let them have their fill of water and allowed them all to breathe and settle themselves before he started to talk.

"Right guys. First thing first. Pride. When we play we play as hard as we can. We play with pride. We do ourselves justice. So, every last one of you – I want you to raise your heads – because we don't ever let our heads go down. Vicky, Liam, Paddy, Shane – let me see those chins higher. Now – that's better – we are Ballincastle and we play with pride in our jersey. We never give up. We play right until the final whistle sounds. Now – we have been here before and we know what to do. Don't we?"

There was a muted response and some dropping of the heads.

"Guys - we have been here before and we know what to do. Don't we?"

This time there was a much more determined response.

"Right – remember the advantage that we have in this position. Carrigleann think they are cruising. They have a six-point advantage and they are feeling good about themselves. And once that second half starts that is when they are most vulnerable. You are going to come out for the second half as if there is only ten minutes left in the match and you are going to give it everything you've got. Empty the tank. Like before – you don't worry about having enough energy to last the game. That's my job. I'll empty the bench after ten minutes if I have to. I'll watch for your energy levels. All you have to agree to is to play these next ten minutes as if you only have ten minutes left in you. And remember – in thirty minutes from now – one team will go home, and one team will go to a Ski na Skull final in Park E. Ring. Who wants to go to Park E. Ring?"

The roar was deafening.

The 'Carrig' team immediately all looked around from their team talk to see where this roar was coming from. The Ballincastle crowd fed off their enthusiasm and raised their voices in support of their team. The team took to their positions and their heads were much higher, their chests pushed out and their eyes firmly focused. The second half started, and Bruce's talk had immediate effect. Ballincastle players were like terriers snapping at the heels of their 'Carrig' opponents. They hassled and harried and shouldered. They turned and ran and sprinted. They soloed and pulled and hooked like their lives depended on the effort.

Within a couple of minutes their efforts were rewarded. They were moving the sliotar so fast Malcolm nearly ran into the net with the sliotar and almost forgot to palm it into the net. The crowd whooped and clapped and cheered. Ballincastle were back in the hunt. The players immediately started to sprint back to their positions for the puck out. There was intensity in their eyes. They were fired up to the hilt. The 'Carrig' goalkeeper was just about to puck out the sliotar when the referee stood in his way and stopped the resumption of play. The referee went over to consult with his umpires. A couple of minutes passed and then the referee instructed the umpire to cross his green and white flags. What!

The goal was disallowed. The referee started to run back from the goal.

"No goal. No goal. Not permitted to palm a goal. No goal."

Oh no. All that for nothing. A couple of players looked at Malcolm with frowns. There was annoyance in their body language. Vicky didn't even know that you couldn't palm the sliotar into the net. Whatever else happened they needed to keep playing as a team. And they needed to keep up the pressure when they had 'Carrig' rocked.

"No fault Malcolm. Absolutely no fault. Come on guys. We are going to get that goal back and we are going to do it now."

The 'now' came as a shout, as an order, as a battle cry. From the puck out the Ballincastle players swarmed around any 'Carrig' player in possession of the sliotar and while 'Carrig' managed to get it down the pitch it was like the ball was too hot to handle. All they wanted to do was to get away from the groups of marauding Ballincastle players and eventually the ball found its way back into Ben's hand to puck out from the Ballincastle goal after a weakly fired wide shot.

Ben surveyed his options – long, short, center, wings. He saw that the players were spread wide and that there was a big space in the middle of the park. He drove it straight up and it bounced in front of Kate. By the time she had collected it and settled herself there was an army of 'Carrig' players descending on her. She raised her head and saw that they had left the wing unattended. As they converged on her she delivered a sweet flick over their heads to Paddy who was steaming down the wing. 'Carrig' were ball watching – about five players started trying to head off any line that Paddy might take on goal. But he didn't. He led them towards the corner. And just when they were all wrong footed, he pulled it straight across the pitch. It was poetic that it should be Malcolm that gratefully received it in front of goal. This time he was not going to make any mistake. The sliotar had top corner written all over before it left his hurley. No withdrawal of the green flag for this one. He punched the air. Ballincastle were back on the track.

The players were not going to give this one up easy. But neither were Carrigleann. In all their intensity Ballincastle were playing on the edge of the rules and it was inevitable that they would start to concede a few frees - and some of these frees were in scoring positions. Within ten minutes of the second half 'Carrig' had been restricted to scoring from frees with nothing from open play. Only problem was that they had notched up three frees so that Ballincastle were back to square one – still two goals or six points behind.

Bruce let them go for another five minutes by which time Ballincastle had snatched another point but, as predicted, the efforts of throwing the kitchen sink at 'Carrig' was starting to show and limbs were getting more tired and reactions slower. Bruce did what he promised. He pretty much emptied the bench, making six substitutions all at the same time. Before the subs went on – and he covered all the outfield sections of center field, halves and full positions – he got all the subs into a huddle.

"Guys – you know what you have to do. You have fifteen minutes. There are a lot of tired Ballincastle guys out there. You need to support them. Even if you have to knock your own guy out of the way – I want you to get your hands on that sliotar. And whatever about tired Ballincastle guys – those Carrigleann guys must be completely wasted by now. Our guys have really put it to them. So, exploit that. Run them ragged. Go for glory. You have absolutely nothing to lose."

These new warriors – Iggy, Jack, Noel, Alan, Damian and Sue – took the field by storm. In every engagement it was clear that they were a second faster, a shoulder stronger, a reaction quicker than their Carrigleann opponents. And slowly it started to show on the scoreboard. The points started to tick over for Ballincastle. Carrigleann still managed to use their skill levels to keep some movements in their scores even though they were physically flagging. But for every point that 'Carrig' scored, Ballincastle were now getting two. And crucially, the frees were now going Ballincastle's way. It was Carrigleann who were really tiring. They were having to resort to chopping and blocking, and from pure tiredness, taking too many steps and even picking up the ball directly with their hands.

All Ballincastle needed was time. But time was running out. Carrigleann were still leading 1-23 to 2-18 and the referee had just started to look at his watch. It was now or never. Sue suddenly found herself in space on the 20-meter line. Sometimes the boys made the mistake of not marking the girls with as much attention as they would the boys. Well, they had made a mistake with Sue – she was more determined than any player on that pitch that they were not going to let this one slip away from them. She had been only on the pitch for fifteen minutes. She felt strong and fresh and could have run for the rest of the day. All the backs had retreated off her. Well - they would pay for that. She kept moving on and on soloing towards the goal. The crowd was literally baying at her to pass it off. She had other ideas. Actually, she only had one idea and she was one hundred percent focused on that idea. She flicked the sliotar in front of her and drew back her hurley and drove it as fast and as hard as she could keeping her head down and keeping the sliotar down.

She didn't see where it went. She didn't have to. The crowd told her. The pained expression on those Carrigleann defenders who had held off her also told her. Served them right. The cheers of her weary teammates said the same thing. The Carrigleann goalkeeper feverishly tried to untangle the sliotar from the net and puck it out as fast as he could but even as the ball flew through the air the referee blew his longest whistle of the day. It was over. It was unreal. How could a small school like Ballincastle make it to the final? The parents went mad. The players went mental. It was embraces and hugs and kisses all around. Even Bruce allowed himself a wry smile. Pairc Ui Rinn, Park E. Ring. Whatever. It was time for celebration.

CHAPTER 12.

All the team said that they would regroup for a WHATSAPP text session that night at the usual time of 7.30pm. As it happened there wasn't that many who got together. The game had drained many of the players both mentally and physically. On the bus back to the school – even though there was wild madness and elation for the first few kilometers of the journey - some of them actually went for a little snooze on the latter section of the journey.

Ben started the WHATSAPP session...

Ben: "Who out der?"

Replies came from Vicky, Noel, Paddy and Iggy.

Vicky: "Wot a game, eh?"

Iggy: "We wuz brill".

Paddy: "We wuz more dan brill. We wuz totesamazeballs"

Noel: "Totesamazesballs boy!"

Vicky: "Know sayin obvious. But we're in final. Yahoo."

Ben: "Pairc Ui Rinn here we come."

Iggy: "Any1 no who we playin?"

Paddy: "Who cares. We'll beat any1."

Noel: "Doncaster United I'd say."

Vicky: "Don't b a clown."

Ben: "I heard it'll b Corramor."

Iggy: "OMG. Dey huge skool. Size of city."

Paddy: "Bigger dey are..."

Iggy: "Serious. Dis is 1 mega skool. No messin here."

Ben: "We got dis far. We shudnt fear any1."

Vicky: "Ben's rite. We in final. 1 team has to win."

Paddy: "Datz what a final means OK..."

Noel: "Smart boy. Smart girl."

Ben: "Guys. Can't keep eyes open. Gotta go to crib. C u 2morrow."

CHAPTER 13.

For the next week all the talk was Sciath na Scol. No matter where you went – in the school, in the town, in the Co-Op, in the shops, even in the city – all the talk was about this school hurling team who were decked out in black and who did a HAKA before their games. The local papers carried two full pages of color photos of the team; of the play in the game and of the crowd on the sidelines. For the Friday edition, the 'Examiner' had picked up on the story. By Saturday the other national papers were carrying the story and the 'RTE Six-One News' on Sunday had a thirty second slot given over to this HURLING HAKA story. The HAKA angle had really taken the imagination of the newshounds. By the following week even a New Zealand channel – TVNZ – had carried the story.

It would be a bit of an exaggeration to say that the news item had gone viral but there were not many rural schools who could say that their build up to the final was featured on TV news channels and channels as far away as New Zealand. Certainly, in the local area the team had achieved a brief celebrity status. As the boys or girls on the team walked around about their usual business, they would notice people pointing them out as one of the 'HAKA team'.

But there was another group who were also very much aware of this newfound notoriety and not at all happy about it. At the final training session before the final, Bruce went through his now usual set of training routines followed by a practice match and then he got them all together for a final briefing. Everybody was expecting a rousing speech to send them on their way home with fire in their bellies. They weren't expecting what came next.

Bruce took a letter from his pocket and waved it in front of him.

"Guys - I got a letter forwarded on to me today from the school."

Everybody's first thought was that this was from the Parents Association or the School Management Committee wishing them luck in the final.

"It is from the Gaelic Athletic Association Cork County Board. They forbid the team to perform any HAKA in advance of the final in Park E. Ring. They request the team to revert to their previous blue colored jerseys."

This was a complete surprise. You could have heard a falling pin travel to the ground. No-one said anything for a minute. There was a total silence. Each person looked around at the next looking for a reaction, looking for a direction. No-one spoke for ages. Finally, Jack asked:

"So, what do we do?"

Bruce looked around at each of them.

"There is nothing we can do. Except go along with what they say.

I've asked about this. The County Board has timed this letter so that we haven't sufficient time to challenge their decision, even if we wanted to do that. I guess its blue jerseys and no HURLING HAKA for the final."

"Ah no."

"No way."

"Why have they done this?"

"This is a balls."

"What's wrong with them?"

"Come on Bruce – this is a joke. It's a wind-up. Tell us now that you are only kidding us?"

"It's no joke guys. Straight up. I'll show you the letter."

They passed the letter from one to the other with little huddles of three or four reading it at the same time. As each group passed it to the next there was a shaking of heads. It was only beginning to sink in.

As the letter made it to the last group Jack broke the long silence.

"OK. So, we just ignore it. Yeah? Business as normal?"

Bruce shook his head.

"I appreciate how you feel guys. But there's two days to the final. We can't contest this. It's a GAA competition. It's their ground. It's their rules. We don't have a choice. It's pretty clear..."

There were blank looks all around.

"...but – listen up guys - we got to the final on skill and determination...and that's what going to bring us the cup on Wednesday. Isn't that right?"

It was just mumbling that came back.

They were meandering off the pitch not really knowing what was happening or what they could do until suddenly Sue turned around and looked directly at Bruce. She had tears of anger in her eyes.

"None of this is right. Nobody cared what we did through three rounds of qualifiers and a semi-final. Now it seems that because we are playing a final in Pairc Ui Rinn suddenly the County Board has to come the heavy. Tell me why it is OK that they feel its right to order us about but not let us ask why. Please – if you can't talk to the County Board – talk to Mr. Fitzpatrick, talk to the Parents Association, talk to the Board of Management. You got us doing the HURLING HAKA. I think we all want to continue...", Sue looked around and there were quiet nodding heads "...talk to somebody. Please. At least ask."

Bruce agreed that there was nothing to lose. He said there would not be time to convene meetings, but he would definitely talk to the principal and as many members of the P.A. and B. of M. as he could. He said not to hold their breaths – he didn't hold out much hope.

Ben had been walking off the pitch and Bruce's words struck a bad chord with him. It was like suddenly he had a rush of blood to the head and it wasn't a nice feeling. His mouth started talking by itself as if he wasn't controlling the words.

"That's crap. You told us not to think that way. You told us we could achieve anything. You told us that we just needed to believe, to give it everything no matter how big the obstacle seemed."

Ben was red from the neck to the forehead, there was a vein throbbing over his eye and his fingers were forming fists and releasing them again as if by their own control. This just wasn't fair.

Bruce looked at him for a moment...

"Touché, Mr. Ben, touché."

Ben kicked a can as he walked to the dressing room ...

"Guys - WHATSAPP - 7.30 - make it happen."

CHAPTER 14.

The HURLING HAKA had gone from a weirdo thing to do to something that defined who they were as a team. This was a disaster. It took some of the good away from getting to the final. Corramor, being a much, much bigger school, had the pick of a massive panel for their team. As seemed to be the case for every game that Ballincastle played – the odds were stacked against them. It would have been nice if they could just smoothly go into the final, doing the things they had been doing, without this County Board thing wrecking their heads. Why wasn't life simple?

At exactly 7.30pm Ben kicked off the WHATSAPP discussion. There was probably the biggest number of players from the team linked into WHATSAPP that evening. Ben scrolled down through the names and reckoned there were twelve typing. Given that some of the panel still didn't have access to WHATSAPP or that their parents kept them away from WHATSAPP, this was a really big turnout.

Ben: "1st things 1st, guys. Wasn't expectin what Bruce said. Do we wanna fight dis? Do we wanna do HURLING HAKA? Or do we roll over on dis 1?"

There was an immediate torrent of "yeses" and "fight, fight, fight".

Ben: "Nybody say no? Dis line will b trouble."

"Fight, fight, fight", the responses came back just like as if it was a schoolyard brawl.

Paddy: "I agree we keep HURLING HAKA. But we need 2 talk bout wot can go wrong here."

Sue: "Wot u mean?"

Paddy: "If we do HURLING HAKA after dey saying 'don't do' – what can dey do to us?"

Sue: "Still don't know what u talkin bout"

Paddy: "Like – could we end up forfeit match.

Sue: "Wot hell does forfeit mean?"

Paddy: "Not play match. Send us back 2 dressin room. Give result 2 Corramor."

Vicky: "De'y'd never do!"

Jack: "Cud de do dat?"

Paddy: "Don't know. But we need 2 know."

Malcolm: "How know?"

Noel: "We read de rule book."

Ben: "Who has copy of rule book?"

Noel: "Don't need copy dummy. Evryting on WWW."

Ben: "Who gonna check it out?"

Noel: "I will. Know it pretty well already."

Vicky: "Nerd. Anorak. Geek."

Ben: "Hey – down girl. This is where we need 2 know the detail. How long u need 2 do Noel?"

Noel: "Bout hour."

Ben: "Back again guys at 8.30pm. Dat OK?"

CHAPTER 15.

Ben had managed to sneak his iPAD down to the bedroom after washing his teeth. These were exceptional circumstances. Noel was right. He was a whiz with the rule book. By 8.30pm he was able to list out all the rules that they could possibly be infringing and what the punishment might be. First thing he said was that if they did any form of the HAKA, it would probably be interpreted as an 'Aggressive Foul'. After that he began to sound like a lawyer or a policeman – listing out the section numbers, the descriptions, and the possible punishment. It was all a bit of a turn off having to listen to Noel go through the rule book section by section. If Mr.

Vance had given this to them as homework, they would have been up in arms that it was too difficult. But even though it was a hard slog, they knew they had to understand what might happen. After thirty minutes of trying to do this over the internet via WHATSAPP, they realized that this wasn't working. They needed to do this face to face. They agreed to do it in the school yard the following day during break time.

Most of the team didn't sleep very well that night. They had learned enough over the WHATSAPP session to worry them. Noel spent a good deal of the night with a torch under the bedclothes getting it all straight in his mind. The following morning, time seemed to slow down it took so long for break time to arrive. Eventually, when it did, they all rushed out to the corner of the yard where Noel held court with his version of what might happen.

If they were to perform any HAKA, then there was a section on 'Aggressive Fouls' which might be what the County Board could use against them. This section had what were described as different category 'Infractions' and there was a different punishment depending on the category of the infraction.

"What the hell – I never knew when I was fouling someone that there were infractions involved. Maybe a fracture if I went in really hard. But 'infractions' is a new one on me", Ted interrupted.

"Shut up Ted, don't be such a smartass. We don't have a lot of time to get this sorted."

The first possible interpretation was that if they performed any HAKA it might be seen as something that fell into "strike or attempt to strike an opponent with an arm, elbow, hand or knee."

"Flippin' hell. We're only doing the HURLING HAKA. It's not as if we are setting up to attack the opposition", Eoin piped up.

"Yeah, yeah. But think like the County Board might think. They don't want us to do this. So, they'll look for every way to stop us. They could say that our waving our arms is like an attempt to hit Corramor players."

"Ah, this is crazy. We'll be nowhere near them."

"County Board are adults remember. You know how they think."

That statement quieted the group and focused the attention.

"So, what's the punishment?"

Noel read from his prepared notes that is was a Category 2 infraction and that the penalty was to order the offender off.

"What – we could all get sent off."

"Don't be silly – how can you get sent off before the game has even started. Dopey."

"'Fraid you're going to have to rewind on that one", Noel cut in very quickly. "Ref can send someone off before the game starts."

"But who would the ref send off – the HURLING HAKA leader, the whole team?"

Everyone was quiet. Nobody knew the answer.

After a while Noel started again.

"OK. There are two different category infractions - To use threatening language to a Referee, Umpire, Linesman or Sideline Official or to use threatening or abusive conduct towards a Referee, Umpire, Linesman or Sideline Official."

Ben was quick off the mark on these infractions – "Right, right – let's not have all the comments that we don't mean to threaten the referee. Once the ref is on the field and if he takes a mind – he can say the HURLING HAKA is threatening language directed at him."

"No argument on that one", agreed Kate, "you can't get much more threatening than a good HURLING HAKA."

That brought a laugh from the group. The sound of a laugh seemed alien – all this serious talk was weird.

"Forget about the abusive conduct", suggested Liam, "if the County Board labelled the HURLING HAKA abusive then there'd be a diplomatic incident with New Zealand".

"Nice one. Ballincastle team the cause of war between Ireland and New Zealand. Tanks on the streets of Cork, snipers hidden in Shandon Bell Tower."

"OK. Let's not lose the run of ourselves here. What's the punishment Noel?"

"Same thing for both – offender ordered off."

The group digested what they had heard so far. There were quick checks on the time as the break time was rapidly eroding away.

"What else you got Noel?"

"Well – there is a category 5 infraction which is similar - To strike or attempt to strike, or any type of assault on, a Referee, Umpire, Linesman or Sideline Official – and again the punishment is the same."

"Anything else?"

"OK – there is a few more - to threaten or to use abusive or provocative language or gestures to an opponent; to threaten or to use abusive or provocative language or gestures to a team-mate; to challenge the authority of a Referee, Umpire, Linesman or Sideline Official. These all merit a caution, but it clearly states that a second offence gets you put off. So, I could easily see a situation that a ref, if he had a mind, could give a yellow card at the start of any form of HAKA and then if you didn't stop turn it into a red card."

"That it, Noel?"

"That's my reading of the rules."

"Great work Noel."

"Yeah – legend."

"Totesamazesballs."

"I couldn't have done that."

"Course you couldn't – you can barely read."

The teachers were herding them all back into the classroom. Before they were separated again Ben hauled them all in tighter.

"Do we all still feel as strongly today as we did last night about going ahead with the HURLING HAKA?"

There were various nods and 'yeahs' and 'bloody right'.

"I've been thinking about it. We're on a collision course here. It smells of trouble. I wouldn't blame anyone for backing out. Call it now if you want out."

No-one spoke.

"I still say it. We shouldn't blame anyone. And something else – if you don't want in but you don't want guys giving you hassle – just pull a sick stomach on the morning of the final. We have to agree not to give anybody who does that a hard time. Your parents won't know any different. They'll just think its nerves. Is that OK guys? Everyone agreed?"

Mr. Vance was breathing down on top of them, wondering why they weren't responding to being called back in and herding them back into the classroom. The looks that exchanged between the hurling team players were determined and defiant.

CHAPTER 16.

The day before the final.

Bruce had organized a final training session for the team. It wasn't meant to be anything serious – just a run out to keep them all limbered up. Usual program – do a few rucks and mauls and passing movements and then get down to a practice game. The practice game wasn't even 'full-on' stuff. Anyone watching could see that players were holding back. Nobody wanted to be the one that got injured the day before the final and miss the biggest day of their sporting life so far – running out in Pairc Ui Rinn in a Sciath na Scol Final.

As the practice game finished up Mr. Fitzpatrick, the Principal, arrived at the side of the pitch. The players congregated around the Coach and the Principal - Mr. Fitzpatrick - cleared his throat and started to speak.

"Boys and Girls, firstly I want to say how proud I am, how proud we all are – teachers, parents, past pupils – that you will be representing the school in the Sciath na Scol Final tomorrow. You have been brilliant and - win, lose or draw tomorrow - you have done a tremendous job and you deserve to feel great about what you have achieved. It's been a long, long time since Ballincastle has been in a Sciath na Scol hurling final and wouldn't it be fantastic for you and the school if you won tomorrow. But whatever happens you boys and girls can hold your heads high."

Mr. Fitzpatrick paused and scanned around looking at each and every one of them.

"I'd also like to take this opportunity to thank Bruce who stepped in at the eleventh hour to take over the coaching duties. At one point it didn't even look like we would be in the competition and now look at us. And while you boys and girls have delivered all the results on the pitch, I know you'd like to join with me to recognize how good a coaching job Bruce has done."

There were cheers and whistles and clapping. Those who could wolf whistle took the opportunity to let out some shrill blasts. Others clashed the ash by knocking hurleys together. It was all smiles and cheers and noise.

Mr. Fitzpatrick continued…"And we know some of Bruce's coaching techniques have been – how do I say it – unconventional."

A couple of sniggers and laughs.

"And those unconventional techniques have attracted a lot of attention – not all of it positive."

No-one was smiling now.

"So, you are all well aware of the edict we got from the County Board. Well – I just want to say that we want to make sure that tomorrow is a very positive day for Ballincastle School. We all, yourselves included, want to see tomorrow as representing all the good things about Ballincastle – your skill, your determination, your 'never-say-die' approach. So, the teaching staff, the Board of Management, the Parents Association, Bruce and myself are all of one mind that we need to go along with what the County Board has indicated. I know you boys and girls can see that this makes sense. Good luck again tomorrow. We are all rooting for you."

And with that he was gone. Scurried off the pitch before anyone could draw breath. And it seemed as if none of the players were drawing breath. There was a silence that was eerie. In fairness to Bruce – he remained in the same position and let things play out. He didn't try to rationalize or apologize. He just – stood there.

In the end it was one of the girls who broke the silence.

"Bruce – we are doing the HURLING HAKA tomorrow", Vicky stated it simply.

Others nodded. It was good to have the HAKA word spoken. Only then was it noticeable that Mr. Fitzpatrick had avoided even saying the word. But still the quietness had a weird feel. Bruce looked around from player to player almost as if he was asking an unspoken individual question of each of them. It seemed like an eternity before he spoke.

"You heard what Mr. Fitzpatrick said, guys."

"Yeah", said Paddy, "but we didn't hear you say anything."

Bruce continued to scan all the faces. It was hard to read him.

"That is factually correct – I didn't say anything."

They waited for him to elaborate but he just stood there. There were a lot of knitted brows and pursed lips among the players. Maybe girls have a better sensitivity towards the unspoken words because Ceara was the one who took up the conversation.

"Maybe you didn't want to say anything?"

"That's possible."

"If you don't say anything you can't tell any lies."

"That's a fact."

"So, there's probably no need to say anything."

"I guess not."

And with that Bruce did more than wish them well for the game on the following day. He told them that they would win. That they had not come this far to lose. That he could see Ballincastle hands on the cup. Then he walked off the pitch.

Malcolm was the first one to speak after Bruce was out of earshot.

"Ceara – what the hell was all that about? I didn't understand a word of what was going on."

"You heard him guys", Ceara replied, "he has given us permission to do the HURLING HAKA. He won't stand in our way."

"You think you heard him say that. What planet are you living on?"

"Venus. And that's why you understand nothing. You are from Mars."

Shane was completely flummoxed. The girls were all smiling. He looked around the rest of the guys.

"I try to understand. She confuses me even further. What's going on here guys?"

Adam didn't want to understand he was only interested in the result.

"Hey – if Ceara heard Bruce say, 'belt away' – that's good enough for me."

This was going to be the last time they would all be together before tomorrow's final. Ben brought them all together into a huddle.

"Guys – I've being thinking about everything Noel told us about the rules. I think I know what's going to happen. I have a plan. You may not like the sound of it but at least it's a plan."

CHAPTER 17

The day of the final.

A couple of months ago this was just a dream. Not one of the team really believed that they would be representing Ballincastle in the Final. The enormity of the day only really began to dawn on the players as the bus pulled into Pairc Ui Rinn and although they were at the ground in lots of time, the crowd was already beginning to build. There was a big support group already there from Corramor. Bigger school, bigger crowd, maybe. The Ballincastle gang was rowdy though. You could hear them from the far stand.

Everybody had bought into Ben's plan. It sounded plausible. His basic idea was that the team would be punished for doing the HURLING HAKA but that there was no way the ref would send everybody off even though they would all be doing the same thing. That would just be OTT. More likely the ref would either book the HURLING HAKA leader under one of the 'dissent' rules or – worse – send the player off under any of the rules they discussed. So that was a potential outcome that they had to accept – if they were to stick to their guns and do the HURLING HAKA – they might be down one player for the whole game. Everyone bought into that risk. Next decision was – who was going to lead the HURLING HAKA – given that they were possibly not going to play. Ben suggested that whoever led would be the captain for the day and then, even if they ended up as non-playing captain, they would have some form of compensation in being photographed with the cup when they won. They tried to get volunteers or to think of clever ways of selecting the HURLING HAKA leader. There were some suggestions that one of the weaker players be chosen so that the loss wouldn't be as keenly felt if the player got sent off. That went down like a lead balloon. Who wants a label as 'captain but weak player'?

In the end they drew straws for it. Nobody could lay their hands on a box of matches, so they spent ages gathering twigs and breaking them down to similar sizes. Each took a twig – one by one. There was fear, suspense, and excitement in the air all at the one time. No player wanted to be the one to draw the short twig for him or herself. Equally – when the playmakers and the rock-solid players were drawing their twigs – players were holding their breaths that none of these would draw the short twig either.

After about twelve players had successfully drawn long twigs Vicky's jaw dropped to the floor when she found herself holding the short twig. She could hardly believe it. She examined the twig almost willing it to grow. There were players coming up and commiserating with her. It was like as if someone belonging to her had died.

"Hey, hey, hold the pony guys", Ben butted in, "there's no guarantee that it will work out like I suggested. Vicky is now our captain. She could be playing. Let's not get ahead of ourselves."

They all agreed and backed off.

Then Vicky shouted at them...

"I will get sent off. Because this is going to be the most aggressive, the most fearsome, the most spine-chilling HURLING HAKA that you have ever seen. The ref will have no option but to send me off."

Everybody laughed. The team was back in business.

That was yesterday. Today sitting in the dressing room in Pairc Ui Rinn it didn't seem all as clear as it looked before. Ben had cleared it with Bruce that Vicky captain the side. Nothing was said about the HURLING HAKA. Equally Bruce passed no comment as he watched the team put on the Black jersey and then cover it by putting the Ballincastle blue jersey over it. He hadn't done his usual team talk in the bus on the way to the match. Maybe it was because they were here in the dressing room so much earlier than they would normally be before a game. Maybe he just wanted to change things around on the big day. Whichever it was, he waited until every last player had done all they needed to do with laces and grips and tapes and helmets and plasters and whatever else made up the ritual of getting ready.

There was fifteen minutes to throw-in, but the teams had to go on the field in the next couple of minutes. This time there would be formal team photographs with newspaper photographers. They would also have to line up before the stand and each player would be individually introduced to the crowd over the loudspeaker system. There were more than a few butterflies in stomachs. No-one had opted out by pulling a sickie. Everyone was in this together.

"Guys – sit down for a few minutes please."

Bruce was the only one who was ice cold calm.

"Vicky is captain for today. Vicky will lead you to victory. I've heard some of you talk Corramor up. They are a big school. They have a massive squad. They are all club players. They won every one of their matches comfortably. Well let me tell you something. They can't hold a candle to you guys. They can't even get near the pride, the determination, the guts, the team spirit that you guys have. Guys – I'd go through a wall for you and I know you'd do the same for each other. When you guys trust yourselves, when you trust each other to back each other up, you can play the most sublime hurling seen in this competition. And when you have your backs to the wall you come out fighting and supporting each other. No other team has that and that's why no other name than Ballincastle will have its name on the cup this year. I want you to do what you've done before. Don't change anything. Give it your all. Don't think any further than half time. Hurl like your lives depend on it. Give it everything. I'm going to give the subs a run whether we're ahead or behind so don't walk off that pitch thinking you could have done more. Give it everything. Go do it."

Vicky led them out on the pitch. If there were butterflies in the stomach before then - there were some weak knees to go with them as well. One stand was entirely full. There was a massive roar. One section was a sea of blue. They ran around and pucked sliotars to each other. Some fired over points. Ben took up a position in goal and got a couple of players to fire shots in at him. Others practiced sideline cuts. After what seemed no time at all they were brought together for the team photo and then lined up for the introduction to the crowd. It was just like a professional sport game. Each player's name was announced and he or she walked a pace forward and waved to the crowd. But for the players it all seemed to go by in a blur.

The referee blew his whistle for the teams to take up their positions. Corramor spread themselves out across the pitch – backs, forwards, midfield.

Vicky assembled the Ballincastle team together close to the halfway line. They took off the blue jerseys. They threw them down on the pitch in defiance. They each took a position at arm's length from each other. Vicky began...

"Ka Mate, Ka Mate..."

CHAPTER 18.

Ka Mate Ka mate

Ka Ora Ka Ora

Ka Mate Ka mate

Ka Ora Ka Ora

Tenei te tangata puru huru

Na'a nei tiki mai whaka whiti te ra

Upane ka upane

Upane ka upane

Whiti te ra

Hi!

Vicky was giving it all she had. The rest of the players fed off her energy. This was shaping up to be the most intense HURLING HAKA they had ever performed. And if there was ever a time to do this, then the middle of Pairc Ui Rinn on Sciath na Scol Final day was definitely the time to pull it out. However, as they predicted – the referee had obviously been primed and was expecting this. No sooner had Vicky started the first quiver of her hands and the ref was up in her face. He said something but, with the intensity of the HURLING HAKA, neither Vicky nor any the rest of the team could actually hear what he was saying. From his body language it was probably something like – 'Stop this now'. Vicky just continued what she had to do and stared him straight in the eye. By the time she was halfway through leading the HURLING HAKA everybody could see the ref reaching into his pocket for a card. Vicky and the rest of the team watched his every tiny movement to see what color would come out. Red and Ballincastle would play the game with fourteen players. Yellow and it might only be a stay of execution to be followed by a red.

There were almost a few weak smiles when the ref put a yellow card almost in Vicky's face. It didn't distract her.

Ka Ora, Ka Ora...

It also didn't change the uneasy look on the Corramor player's faces. Sneers had quickly changed to puzzled looks and were now replaced by some very nervous fumbling with their hurleys. This was a big occasion for every player of this age – the addition of the HAKA was definitely having the anticipated effect of making the Corramor girls and boys more nervous.

Vicky was getting closer to the end.

"Upane Ka Upane..."

The ref still stood there almost in her face. Worryingly, he had his hands in his pockets. Was he going to leave them there or was he going to wait for the dramatic finish of Vicky jumping into the air and then present her with the dreaded red card? It built quickly up to the climax. Vicky launched herself into the air.

"Hi !"

To jump she had to move her whole body forward. As she landed, she came with her feet square on the ground and ended up almost nose to nose with the ref. He looked at her for what was only a couple of seconds but seemed like minutes – both to Vicky and the rest of the team. There was a communal holding of breath. The ref took a step backwards and with one very shrill blast of his whistle ran to where the Corramor center field players were nervously waiting.

Brilliant. They had escaped without Vicky being sent off. Just a yellow card. Really the best they could have hoped for. But one thing they hadn't legislated for. The ref ran to the center of the pitch, blew his whistle again and dropped the sliotar at the feet of the Corramor centre field players. Ballincastle had been in a huddle close to the middle of the field. They were all out of position. Ben was half a pitch sprint away from his goal and as soon as he saw what was in the referee's mind, he started running madly back to the goal area. He hadn't a hope. The Corramor center field just tapped it up to the full forward who gladly flicked it into an open goal.

One goal down on ten seconds. With all their previous discussion and trying to second guess the referee's reactions and his interpretation of the rules, they hadn't included this scenario. The referee was perfectly entitled to start the game. He had given Ballincastle the indication to take their positions on the pitch; they had made the decision to group together to perform the HURLING HAKA. This was the ref making a statement – 'I control the game, guys, not you." So, the punishment was a goal down as well as the yellow card.

Some heads went down more at the stupidity of not anticipating this than anything else. Vicky started to play her role as captain. She shouted up and down the pitch.

"No worries. We just start playing from now. With fifteen players, lads, with fifteen players. "

The message was clear. They were ahead of their worst-case scenario. It would be easier to get the goal back over the course of the entire game than to play for an hour with one player less. It settled the squad a bit to have it said so clearly. And they needed to settle. Because straight from Ben's puck out Liam made a very uncharacteristic error in not securing possession and a Corramor player pounced on the sliotar and put it straight back over the bar. A couple of minutes down and they had gifted Corramor 1-1.

And for the next fifteen minutes it didn't get much better. It wasn't necessarily that Ballincastle weren't playing well – no – that wasn't the case. They were managing to compete quite well given that all the Corramor players seemed, to a girl and boy, to be a head taller. But the decision-making just didn't seem to be coming off for them. On a number of occasions where points would have been easy to pick off, it seemed to the attacking player that a goal opportunity was available. But for one reason or another it didn't work out. After fifteen minutes all Ballincastle had to show for their efforts were two points from frees. They hadn't scored anything from play. Corramor, on the other hand seemed to be picking off points at ease and kept their side of the scoreboard ticking over. Being down 1-8 to 0-2 after fifteen minutes was not part of the game plan and, if anything, seemed to make the Ballincastle decision making even worse. The players were feeling the need to go for goal to compress the score difference as quickly as possible.

Rewards were scant. Although Shane did rattle the net before half time and Ballincastle picked off a couple of extra points, Corramor seemed to be scoring much freer and with much less effort. It was a very tired and downhearted Ballincastle team who retreated to the dressing room staring at a mountain of a score that gave Corramor 2-12 to Ballincastle 1-4. There were players dragging tired limbs and low spirits. A number of them would have already resigned themselves to runners up medals and thinking that it was all over. It was a strange experience to be in a dressing room at half time – every other game they had played it was just a matter of finding a place on the field to get into a huddle. But this was Pairc Ui Rinn. This was different. Players sat on the bench all around the dressing room with heads down not wishing to look anyone else in the eye.

Bruce read the mood to a tee. He didn't say anything at first just went around distributing water bottles. He knew he had ten to fifteen minutes which was way more that most halftimes when teams don't retreat to the dressing room. He knew, because of this extra rest period, that he needed to time his talk 'just right'. He moved from player to player praising each one's individual efforts and giving some advice as to how they could better mark their opponent, how they could better beat their opposition, how they could correct some of their approaches. All the time he was very conscious to not criticize but to keep everything positive.

In a way he had nothing new to say. They had been in this position a number of times already. They had to take advantage of the smugness in the other teams' dressing room in the first couple of minutes of the second half. They had to score first. They had to build on that. They had to swing the balance in their favour. He could get their heads back up and he could change their mood – he knew he could do that. He could get them spitting blood before they went back on the pitch – he knew he could do that. But did he keep the same team out there for the second half or did he ring the changes? That was what he was mulling over in his mind as he started to talk to them.

"Listen up guys. Listen up. Heads up. I want to look each one of you in the eye."

Bruce made a dramatic slow walk around the dressing room making eye contact with each player.

"How many games have we been in this position? How many games have we gone out into the second half and ground out the win by wearing the opposition down?"

It didn't really need an answer. Everyone remembered the games. Nobody answered in any event.

"Why did we succeed? We succeeded because we believed. Because we knew if we play our hearts out and support one another that we will win. But that's easy to say. We have to be clear now in the next few minutes what it really means. And this is what it means. Every time there is a Corramor player in possession there will be three of you surrounding him. Every time someone of us moves in defence or attack you will move too in support. Every time you are in possession of the sliotar you won't even have to look – there will be someone supporting to the left and to the right and behind and straight ahead. Every time you hit the ground you will be thinking of getting up as quickly as possible to move into the next position. Every time you score, you'll punch the air like you know it's just the start of the next score. Everyone else will cheer you. Any time you miss you'll forget it and move your mind to the next attack. Everyone else will shout 'no fault'. You'll run every move like it's a hundred-meter sprint. There is one half left of this final. You won't even consider conserving energy. You will run your hearts out for your fellow player. I will watch you. I will sub you when your tank hits empty. It's one half guys. One half to grab the trophy. No use tomorrow wondering what might have been, reliving some ifs, buts and maybes. Corramor are at their most vulnerable now. You can severely rattle their cage. But you have to do it together and you have to do it from the 'off'. Now do you know what it means?"

This time the response was at ear splitting decibels. Bruce wondered whether he himself had got the balance right. Sometimes you can concentrate so much on passion that the clarity and coolness of decision-making goes out the window and the whole thing works in reverse. Cold blue passion was always what he aimed for. Red hot aggression didn't often win the day. Anyway, it was done now. He had to trust his instincts. He then made his last half time decision.

"Guys – there is absolutely nothing wrong with the way you are playing. So, the team stays the same for the start of the second half."

Some of the subs looked crestfallen. Everybody was wound up like a coiled spring and just wanted to get the game restarted.

"But I will be making some early substitutions. And everybody is going to get a run no matter what the situation. This is the final of the Ski Na Skull competition and each squad member is going to be able to say that they played their part in the victory. Now. Go do it."

The clash of studs on the short concrete pathway out to the grass of the pitch seemed to echo more loudly as the team rushed out onto the pitch, hurleys in hand, wanting the whistle to sound so that they could do battle. This time there was no delay with taking positions on the pitch and each boy and girl had taken their place well ahead of the Corramor team. The crowd supporting both teams roared them on and there was an air of electricity as the ref threw the sliotar along the ground between the competing center field players.

If Bruce wanted an immediate response – he got it. Kate shouldered the boy who was marking her squarely and fairly and left him in a heap on the ground as she cleanly picked up the sliotar on her hurley and rifled it down to the forward line. The ball drifted off towards the corner of the field, but Eoin took his opposite number by surprise by pulling directly on the ball like a sideline cut and floating it in towards the goal. Fionn left his marker for dust and met it on the volley and before Corramor knew the match had restarted the sliotar was in the back of the net. Goal !

Vicky was punching the air more than Fionn.

"Corramor got their free goal in the first half. That one is ours. It doesn't stop here guys."

The Ballincastle crowd really got behind the players. They roared and screamed and shouted. You could just about pick out the screaming of the younger schoolchildren and the exhortations of the parents as it all blended together in a wall of sound. 2-4 to 2-12 put a slightly different perspective on the scoreboard but there was still a significant matter of an eight-point gap. There was a long way to go in the second half but there was a big mountain to climb. Bruce silently and subconsciously flexed and unflexed his fists by his side. Yes! It was a start. It was a perfect start. Now he needed to do his job and mind each player individually. Watch them all. Make sure that each one still had the energy to contribute to the team. And fulfill his promise that everyone could get a run.

Bruce had been absolutely spot-on about the start of the second half being the vulnerable time for the leading team. Corramor didn't have the swagger they had in the first half. They managed to push over a couple of points but then Ballincastle had a purple patch a few minutes later. After one of the Corramor points Ben had taken a really quick puck out. The Corramor players were still running backwards enjoying their point when Ben picked out Shane on the right wing and delivered it with pitch point accuracy to his hand. Shane pushed it directly up the line to Vicky at half forward. Vicky feigned to drive it in towards the goal and fooled her opponent completely, side stepping him and leaving him flat footed in her wake. The Ballincastle forwards spread out and offered up multiple choices for a pass. Vicky did the clever thing and solo-ed onwards just enough to suck in numerous Corramor defenders. The Ballincastle forwards were queueing up for the sliotar to be passed to them. Any number of them were in good positions. Bruce looked on and willed for them to go for goal. This could be a turning point. They had to start turning their good patches of play into scores on the board. He needn't have worried. Vicky deftly picked out Fionn who, with only the goalkeeper to beat, didn't miss from those kinds of opportunities. The Corramor goalkeeper hardly moved. Fionn had another goal on his personal tally and

Ballincastle moved to within seven points. (3-4 to 2-14)

It didn't stop there. The Corramor half back who collected the puck out must have felt the sliotar came to him with a big red cross on it. He was surrounded by Ballincastle players who hustled the ball away from him. A couple of accurate passes and this time Eoin found himself in a similar position with only the 'keeper to beat. He swung on it with all his might. It had goal written all over it. The crowd was already cheering in anticipation. But instead of rippling the net it ricocheted savagely off the top side of the crossbar and almost vertically into the air. But while Corramor players were standing around watching where it might land, three or four black shirts were zeroing in. It was Liam whose hurley stretched highest and from almost underneath the cross bar he deflected it into the corner and well away from the flailing goalkeeper who was struggling with all the Ballincastle attention.

Now things were getting serious. Some of the Corramor coaches were turning purple in the face because they were shouting at their players so forcibly. Bruce was quietly trying to contain himself and let his team do their talking on the pitch. At 4-4 to 2-14 and the margin decreased now to four points, Bruce was silently urging his guys to keep up the pressure. Ballincastle had done exactly what he had asked them to do and could keep Corramor on the run. But if they allowed them back into this game then it was equally possible that Corramor could run away again like they had in the first half. He must have looked a strange sight on the sideline often scanning directly away from the point of play trying to make sure he took in all the signs of tiredness in the players whether on or off the sliotar.

The next passage of play saw Corramor and Ballincastle trade points in equal measure. First one team would fire over a point then the other. This too and fro went on for at least fifteen minutes. There was no quarter given or taken. There were highly physical exchanges and whether boy or girl didn't ever come into it, it was full-on play with the focus of getting the upper hand advantage. Bruce made a number of substitutions through the second half as he saw players begin to tire. In fairness to the new legs that came on – every one of them had brought new energy and spirit to the team.

With eight minutes to go Bruce began to have the horrible thought that maybe they would run out of time. A number of players had been leading the charge and really playing to the top of their capability. However, a number of these were now flagging and needed to come off. They had given everything they possibly could but were literally out on their feet. Bruce readied the last of the subs. In one substitution switch he took off Paddy, Liam, Tadhg, Fionn, Kate and Iggy. He knew by the look on their faces that none of them wanted to come off. In normal circumstances any of these guys were capable of turning a game. He knew that taking them all off together must look like a suicide decision. But he knew he didn't have a choice. They had all literally run themselves into the ground. This was it. The last throw of the dice. This would probably be a contradiction of the longest and shortest eight minutes ever.

The newbies knew that they only had minutes and gave it everything. Sue, who had never played in a full forward position before, marked her entry to the game with the most sublimely taken point from out near the touchline. But Corramor were still strong and had kept their shape. A couple of points were traded, and the game now started to see a lot more wides than before as players on both sides visibly tired. With two minutes to go and only three points in it there was always the hope of a Ballincastle goal to keep the game alive. But it was difficult to see where it was going to come from with all the Ballincastle playmakers now on the sideline. The vigor and determination were etched on the players faces as they still challenged for every opportunity. Such a challenge forced something from a hopeless situation. Sue was using her fresh legs to chase a Corramor defender who had cleanly picked the sliotar. He clumsily dropped it and then panicked by Sue's attention he put it out over his own end line.

Eoin ran straight to the '45' to take responsibility. With hardly anything left on the clock this was a lifeline. He knew what he had to do. Drive it high and into the square and allow Ballincastle players the best opportunity to turn it into the goal. That would even the scores and keep them in the game. Maybe force it to extra time and then anything still could happen. He looked at the goal, gripped his hurley, lifted the sliotar and drove it in a high lob towards the goal. He watched it soar. The direction was good. He held his breath. The ball could not have been aimed better – it was in a direction towards the middle of the goal. He watched it start to dip. What had he done? It wasn't dipping quickly enough. There was a massive scramble in the goalmouth box of upraised hurleys but the sliotar went above the highest of these and slipped over the bar. Oh no. Any other day he would have been proud as punch at putting one right between the posts. But this was a failure. There could only be seconds left. There was still two points between the teams.

The Corramor goalkeeper was moving like a geriatric trying to chew up as much time as he could. The referee was looking at his watch. He wasn't too impressed with the blatant timewasting. He motioned for the Corramor 'keeper to puck it out. Still the 'keeper delayed - walking left and walking right as if selecting his target. The ref continued to wave him on, waving each time with more annoyance. Finally, the keeper pucked it out. But in trying to gain as much territory up the field he didn't make a clean connection and it scuttered out to the right where a surprised Adam saw the sliotar scurry along the grass in front of him. He dived forward to try and lift it into his hand. As he tried to get a clean lift, he was surrounded by five Corramor players. They were trying to make sure they recovered possession at all costs and get it down the field. Adam got the sliotar into his hand but with all the pressure, lost it again. He kept battling for the ball despite the pressure. The ball was on the ground, but he was completely surrounded. He didn't even have sufficient elbow room to lift his hurley. Despite all the Corramor players surrounding him, out of the corner of his eye he spotted Eoin completely unmarked about ten meters away. With only a tiny bit of room to move his hurley back, he flicked the sliotar through the mass of legs. It didn't travel far but at least cleared the melee of players and went in Eoin's direction.

Eoin stretched out his hurley and lifted the sliotar cleanly from the grass into his hand while at the same time pivoting on his heel and moving towards the goal. A corridor to the goal had opened up for him. All the Corramor defenders had been surrounding Adam. Eoin was still about thirty meters from the goal but he had a head start on the defence. He was on a solo mission. He bore down on the goal. He knew this was the absolute last chance. Twenty-five meters. Twenty meters. He was still clear of defenders but could hear them bearing down on him. He could see the 'keeper bracing himself to come out and narrow the angle. Eoin needed to make a decision as to when to fire in on goal. He flicked the sliotar into his hand. This was it. He was going for it.

Next thing Eoin knew his face was in the grass. One of the Corramor players had blatantly taken the legs from under him. Eoin heard a shrill blast of the whistle. On the ground he didn't know whether the ref had blown for full time. A couple of his teammates lifted an arm each and dragged him to a standing position. He looked around. The referee was pointing for a free on the 20-meter line. The Corramor defenders were already packing the goal line. Eoin brushed himself off and got ready to tee up the sliotar. Vicky rushed up to the 20-meter line.

"No. No. Ben is taking this."

The players looked at each other not knowing what was going on.

"Ben, Ben", Vicky and others shouted down to the goalkeeper. "Get yourself up here quickly."

Ben ran the whole length of the pitch. He was breathless by the time he reached the opposition 20-meter line.

"What's going on?" he shouted.

"You take it Ben. Do a 'Nasher' on it."

"What? I've never done it before in a match."

"I've watched you practice", Vicky encouraged, "I know you can do it. I know you are the right person to do it."

Ben placed the sliotar the way he wanted it on the 20-meter line. He was still breathing deeply from running the whole length of the pitch. The referee was asking him to get on with it. This was the last strike of the game. A goal would give Ballincastle the game by a single point. Anything less and the cup would go to Corramor. Vicky wanted Ben to take the free in the way that Anthony Nash had made famous. It amounted to lifting the sliotar in such a way that you flicked it high and way out in front of you so that effectively you were meeting the ball a number of meters in front of you. Flick it up well and you had the advantage of being much closer to goal when you fired it in. Flick it up poorly and you risked not controlling the shot. It looked easy when it was well done but it wasn't easy to master.

"I'm going to have to ask you to take the free, son."

The referee was getting impatient.

Through the sharp, short intakes of breath Ben could hear the crowd going positively mental. The Ballincastle supporters were urging the sliotar into the net. The Corramor crowd was doing their upmost to put Ben off.

It was now or never. Ben could hear his heart pounding in his ears. He lifted the sliotar in a high arc and moved forward to meet it. He had flicked it way ahead of him, maybe further than he was comfortable with. He started the swing of his hurley. He was going to give this everything he had. The Corramor defenders were dancing on the line not knowing where the sliotar was going to go. Ben met it hard but not square on. He had meant to drive it towards the roof of the net but he ended up driving it low. The Corramor defenders and goalkeeper were completely confused. Ben's eyes and body movement told them it was going high. They didn't have time to readjust. One of them drew out a despairing boot as the sliotar planted itself in the bottom corner of the net.

Goal !

The referee blew three long blasts on the whistle.

Ben fell to his knees holding the hurley in his two hands above his head.

Bruce ran onto the pitch. The substituted players ran onto the pitch. The Ballincastle crowd ran onto the pitch. Everyone was jumping, hugging, and punching the air. Legend.

EPILOGUE.

The picture of Ben on his knees with the hurley above his head and an expression that spoke of happiness, relief, determination and exhaustion was the one that covered half of the front page of the "Irish Examiner" the following day. It was a journalists dream – the underdogs; the small school; the New Zealand coach; the All Blacks shirts, The HURLING HAKA, the controversy with the County Board; the dramatic manner of the victory and now this magnificent photo of the winning scorer. The Ballincastle Sciath na Scol hurling team knew that they had accomplished something brilliant for themselves and for their school. And boy – were they enjoying it. What they didn't realize was that they had accomplished something unique.

The big banner headline above the "Irish Examiner" picture was 'HAKA Hurlers'. And that was the name that went viral across the media. The story of the HAKA Hurlers' victory in the final captured the imagination of the media and the story was played out in print, TV and radio in the UK, in the USA, in Canada in Australia and of course in New Zealand.

For many years afterwards if someone said they went to school in Ballincastle, the next predictable question was – 'were you one of the HAKA hurlers?". Or if the age profile didn't fit – 'did you know anyone on the HAKA hurling team? The exploits of that Under Twelve Sciath na Scol hurling team were known far and wide.

There was a vicious rumour directly after the final that the County Board were going to make the result of the final null and void because of Ballincastle's failure to align with the express direction they had been given not to perform the HURLING HAKA. It was never confirmed whether or not this was true. Others contended that it was definitely true and that the only reason they didn't go through with it was all the worldwide publicity the final achieved. They knew there would be a savage adverse backlash if they took the victory away from Ballincastle.

One item which was definitely true was that the next Annual Congress of the GAA had a motion before it to 'prohibit premeditated acts of team aggression before a match'. The motion was defeated. Not because people supported actions like the HURLING HAKA – quite the opposite. But the debate became over-philosophical with counties arguing that a dressing room warm-up could become banned under the rule. The HURLING HAKA incident faded into history; wasn't repeated by other teams and no other similar motion came before Congress.

Bruce returned to New Zealand not long after the final. He needed to return to a family gathering back home and ended up never returning. He still drops the odd note to Mr. Fitzpatrick and last heard he was back coaching a school team again – but no – not Gaelic Games – Rugby Union.

A re-union takes place every year for the Ballincastle HAKA Hurlers. They come from far and wide.

Acknowledgements

I would never have written this story were it not for the motivation provided by my son, Ben. But it came in a slightly different form than I was expecting. 'Why don't you write about things that interest me?', he asked – 'none of the topics you've written about so far are things that me and my friends relate to'. Wow! Thanks for that Ben. Well – OK. So, I turned it into a positive idea. He – GAA/hurling, me - Rugby. Thus, the marriage of ideas.

Therefore, the first people I need to thank are my son Ben and my brother Jack. They know much more about hurling and GAA than I ever will, and they made sure that any hurling statements were correct. Thank you, guys. Thanks also to my wife Helena and sister Anne for the editing and precise proof-reading.

On the artistic side – great work again by Caoimhe Walsh for the design and artwork of the cover. Thanks to Ollie Murray for all the formatting work.

It is great to be able to share a winning moment – doesn't matter whether you play, coach or support from the sidelines. But even if one never wins – sport is brilliant. It bonds people together with a common interest and lifts everything up another level. It makes the thoughts turn quicker and the heart pump faster. Hopefully 'HURLING HAKA' conveyed some of this.